A *Journey* OF *Repentance, Renewal,* AND *Return*

R.E. HASSELBACH

A Journey of Repentance, Renewal, and Return

This book is written to provide information and motivation to readers. Its purpose is not to render any type of psychological, legal, or professional advice of any kind. The content is the sole opinion and expression of the author, and not necessarily that of the publisher.

Printed in the United States of America.

ISBN   978-1-955363-26-6   (Paperback)
ISBN   978-1-955363-27-3   (Digital)

Lettra Press books may be ordered through booksellers or by contacting:

Lettra Press LLC
30 N Gould St. Suite 4753
Sheridan, WY 82801
1 307-200-3414 | info@lettrapress.com
www.lettrapress.com

Contents

This book is dedicated to my parents, Alfred and Madeleine Hasselbach, whose love and faith first led me to Christ; to the Franciscan friars of Holy Name Province, who formed my faith as a young man; to the people of the Clarkstown Reformed Church, whose faith and prayers sustain me every day, and, with love, to my lifelong friend Paula.

Introduction

Lent and the God of Second Chances

Lent is about repentance, change, and starting over. It's about second chances.

On December 23, 1849, a small group of prisoners was taken from Peter and Paul Fortress, a maximum-security prison in St. Petersburg, Russia, and brought to Semyonov Square in St. Petersburg to be executed by firing squad. For eight months these condemned men had lived in deplorable conditions for the crime of being critical of the Tsar. After being given the opportunity to confess to a priest, each had a black hood placed over his head and was readied for execution. The soldiers aimed their rifles, waiting for the command to shoot.

Do you think these doomed prisoners were worse sinners than all other Russians? I tell you they were not! But unless you repent, you will likewise perish.

On the road to his own execution, Jesus encountered people gossiping about an atrocity committed by Pontius Pilate when he ordered his solders to kill some Galileans who had gone to the Jerusalem Temple to offer sacrifice. We don't know more about this incident, but we do know Pilate was a brutal man, quick to move from diplomacy to violence.

In the theology of the time, suffering was accepted as punishment for sin. There was something oddly comforting about this belief; when there is a reason for suffering, it is more manageable and less random. Those who suffer "had it coming." Jesus rejects this theory in short order: the Galileans killed by Pilate in the temple were no more sinful than all the other residents of Galilee; the eighteen people killed when the tower of Siloam collapsed were similarly not worse sinners than all the other people in Jerusalem. Jesus cautions, "But unless you repent, you too will all perish" (Luke 13:5).

The Lord is not saying that repentance will somehow ward off all human or natural evil. Rather, he underscores the urgency of repentance. Every one of the people killed by Pilate, or by the tower collapse, started their day routinely. Like the victims of the 9/11 attack on the World Trade Center, they ate their breakfast, kissed their kids, and headed off to start their day. In their wildest imagination, they never thought they would die, but death came suddenly, unexpectedly, like a thief in the night. It is impossible for us to imagine our own non-being, so, regardless of our age or physical condition, we think we will at least live to see tomorrow. For the Galileans murdered in the temple, or the eighteen crushed by the tower, or the victims of 9/11, there was no tomorrow, nor was there time to make peace with God or anyone else. Here is the reason for Jesus's urgency: unless we repent *now*, we will perish as they did: unprepared.

Jesus was a Jew speaking to Jews. When he stresses the importance of repentance, he is thinking of the Hebrew concept of *teshuva*, which means to turn, or return. Repentance, in this sense, is to turn away from sin and to return to living in obedience to God.

Teshuva is more than feeling sorry for sin. First, we must do a fiercely honest examination of our lives—before we repent, we must know we are sinners. How have we broken faith with God or others? Who have we betrayed; how have we fallen short; in what ways have we lost our integrity or strayed morally? This inner work is a necessary starting point for repentance. When people discover their flaws, they often look for someone to blame, but teshuva requires us be accountable. We—no one else—are responsible for our own sinfulness. Teshuva requires that we look for ways to make amends for the damage our sin has caused.

Understood as Jesus meant it, repentance holds out the possibility that we can be fully reconciled to God and to our communities; change our lives; and that even our flaws can be sanctified. There is no brokenness that God cannot transform into something beautiful when we trustingly place it before him. We can do none of this by ourselves. We need God's help; we need a savior.

To illustrate that God is a God of second chances, Jesus gives us the parable of a fig tree that has not been fruitful for three years. The owner of a vineyard, disappointed by his barren tree, tells his gardener to cut it down. The gardener, however, unwilling to give up on the tree, urges the owner to "leave it alone for one more year, and I'll dig around it and fertilize it" (Luke 13:8). The Greek word for "leave it alone" is *aphes*, which means "forgive." Forgive the tree, he pleads, so that he can have time to nourish and nurture the it, providing the failing tree with that which it could not provide for itself. Presumably, if the tree did not bear fruit in a year the gardener would again ask for *more* forgiveness: recall that when Peter asked the Lord how many times he should forgive another the Lord told him to place no limits whatsoever on his forgiveness: "I tell you, [forgive] not seven times but seventy times seven times" (Matthew 18:22). There is still urgency, though. Every moment we waste on sin is a moment lost to life.

Back in Semyonov Square, just before they were to be executed, the prisoners heard a drumroll and the sound of beating hooves. A messenger came from the Tsar commuting the death sentence to a term of four years hard labor in Siberia.

Twenty years later, in his novel *The Idiot*, Fyodor Dostoevsky wrote about a twenty-seven-year-old character, waiting, as Dostoevsky once did in that square in St. Petersburg, to be executed. "What if I didn't have to die?" the character asks. "I would turn every minute into an age, nothing would be wasted, every minute would be accounted for."

God gives us every chance we need. Are we making every minute count? Are we living life, as he would have us live it, to the full? Have we made use of our second chances?

Chapter 1

Ash Wednesday through Saturday

Ash Wednesday
Scripture Reading

Rend your heart
and not your garments.
Return to the Lord your God,
for he is gracious and compassionate,
slow to anger and abounding in love,
and he relents from sending calamity.
Who knows? He may turn and relent
and leave behind a blessing—
grain offerings and drink offerings
for the Lord your God.
Blow the trumpet in Zion,
declare a holy fast,
call a sacred assembly (Joel 2:13–15).

Reflection

There is a price to pay for sin. In a plague of locusts devouring the land, the prophet Joel saw a portent of God's judgment on sinful Israel. When there is sin, God's punishment will be sure and terrible. Yet Joel was hopeful; there was still time to turn back to God. he urged his countrymen to wake up the reality of their situation; lament the destructive consequences of their sinfulness, and to take action by turning their hearts back to God.

Our nation is torn apart by hatred. We dispose of inconvenient lives and create a culture of death. Once God-fearing, we now have become laws unto ourselves. Our materialism disguises a pathetic spiritual poverty visible in teenage suicides, mass killings, an epidemic of drug and alcohol abuse, broken marriages, and empty lives.

Call a fast! Deny yourself, repent, and turn back to God with all your heart.

Prayer

Creator God, your heart aches when you see our sinful world and sinful lives. We think too much of ourselves and our convenience and too little of you, your justice, and your love. In the name of tolerance, we accept injustice and inhumanity; we are not moved by the plight of the poor, and we turn a blind eye to the holocaust of abortion. Give us wisdom and the spirit of repentance, Lord, so that we might know what is right in your eyes and have the courage to do it. Help us to rend our hearts, deny ourselves, and follow your Son Jesus through these forty days of Lent. He is the one who died and now lives with you forever. Amen.

Activities

This is the first day of Lent.
- Go to church and take ashes. Let those ashes be an outward sign of your honest inward desire to "rend your heart."
- Fast and abstain from meat on Wednesdays and Fridays during Lent. An easy way to fast is to have one full meal (a vegetable, a small starch, and a protein about the size of a deck of cards). Forget about dessert and instead eat two smaller meals, each half the size of the full meal.
- Start a prayer journal, and keep it throughout Lent.
- Pray for the sins of the nation.

Prayer Journal and Notes

_____

_____

_____

_____

_____

_____

_____

_____

_____

_____

_____

_____

_____

_____

_____

_____

_____

_____

Thursday after Ash Wednesday

Scripture Reading

Then [Jesus] said to them all: "Whoever wants to be my disciple must deny themselves and take up their cross daily and follow me. For whoever wants to save their life will lose it, but whoever loses their life for me will save it. What good is it for someone to gain the whole world, and yet lose or forfeit their very self?" (Luke 9:23–25).

Reflection

Following Jesus is no easy matter. Many have walked away from the Gospel because of the message of the cross: "a stumbling block to the Jews and foolishness to the gentiles" (1 Corinthians 1:23). Our culture encourages us to have high self-esteem, be self-possessed, and be self-actualized. Jesus tells us, however, that we need to lose our self-centeredness, and from the cross, he shows us the way. He gives the last drop of his blood to save us, and we can return nothing but our gratitude. Jesus goes to his cross out of love for us and in obedience to his Father. To be his follower, we must, like Jesus, die to ourselves so that we can live to him. That death, in us, takes the form of putting ourselves last—as "the slave of all" (Mark 10:44). It means struggling to extinguish our egos and become of the same mind-set as Christ.

Prayer

Father of our Lord, Jesus Christ, fill us with his spirit so that we might have the mind-set of your Son. He gave of himself while holding nothing back, suffering death on the cross to reveal your unfathomable love for us. Give us the strength and courage to give of ourselves for others, taking on, as he did, the nature of a servant. Give us the wisdom to humbly follow your will in obedience so that, like Jesus, we might reveal your love and reflect your image. We make this prayer in his name and through the power of the Spirit. Amen.

Activities

- Give some of your "stuff" to the poor. If you have two sweaters, give one away. If you have a lot of excess clothing, give it to the poor.
- Do something kind for someone anonymously.
- Volunteer to do something at your church.
- Forgive someone from the heart—wholeheartedly and with no strings attached.

Prayer Journal and Notes

_____

_____

_____

_____

_____

_____

_____

_____

_____

_____

_____

_____

_____

_____

_____

_____

_____

_____

Friday after Ash Wednesday

Scripture Reading

Have mercy on me, O God,
according to your unfailing love;
according to your great compassion
blot out my transgressions.
Wash away all my iniquity
and cleanse me from my sin.
For I know my transgressions,
and my sin is always before me (Psalm 51:1–3).

Reflection

In 1973, the renowned psychiatrist Karl Menninger wrote *Whatever Became of Sin?* In it, he explained how the notion of personal, moral evil has been sanitized and psychologized. Now when people do evil things, society chalks it up to sickness. In the popular mind, even the causes of crime are attributed to social problems: poverty, childhood trauma, ignorance, and so on. For us to experience God's forgiving love, however, we must, to paraphrase the psalmist, know our transgressions and hold our sin always before us.

God has given us the gift of freedom. Each of us can make of the events of our lives a blessing or a curse. We can choose to do good or evil. And when we do harm, we sin. All of us sin—sometimes in small ways and sometimes in significant ways. But all sin is an abomination in the sight of the righteous, kind, and loving God.

Lent is a time to know our transgressions, see our sinfulness, and take all that baggage to the Lord because he is merciful and has great compassion. Only he can blot out our transgressions, wash away our iniquity and cleanse us from our sin. He does that through the blood of Jesus, which was freely shed for us on the cross to wash us clean of all sin and to give us life eternal in his name.

Prayer

Eternal God, look upon me in my sinfulness. I have done what is evil in your sight. I have been cold and unforgiving even though you forgive me so unreservedly. I have hurt the people around me by what I have done and by what I have left undone. I have ignored your presence in my life and lived as if you don't matter. Because of my hardness of heart, I have slipped into habits of sin: I routinely do what is not pleasing in your eyes and am chained to my favorite vices. Only you can forgive me; only you can save me. Wash me clean, saving Father, through the blood of your Son. Free me from all that holds me in its thrall so that I might live in the light of your love and know the joy and freedom that only you can give me. I ask this in Jesus's name. Amen.

Activities

- If you are estranged from anyone, take a few minutes to write him or her a note.
- Start the practice of examining your conscience every evening before you go to bed. Do this at least for the rest of Lent. Note any insights in your "Prayer Journal and Notes."
- Keep a cross or crucifix prominently displayed in your home and office, and let it be a reminder of the high price paid for your (and our) forgiveness.

Prayer Journal and Notes

_____

_____

_____

_____

_____

_____

_____

_____

_____

_____

_____

_____

_____

_____

_____

_____

_____

_____

Saturday after Ash Wednesday

Scripture Reading

After this, Jesus went out and saw a tax collector by the name of Levi sitting at his tax booth. "Follow me," Jesus said to him, and Levi got up, left everything, and followed him.

Then Levi held a great banquet for Jesus at his house, and a large crowd of tax collectors and others were eating with them. But the Pharisees and the teachers of the law who belonged to their sect complained to his disciples, "Why do you eat and drink with tax collectors and sinners?"

Jesus answered them, "It is not the healthy who need a doctor, but the sick" (Luke 5:27–31).

Reflection

Tax collectors were on the margins of Jewish life during the time of Christ. They were wealthy (mostly because they were corrupt), and they worked for the hated Roman overlords. Tax collectors were the traitors of their day; they were despised. When Jesus called a tax collector to follow him, tongues wagged. People said, "Doesn't he know he's just called a sinner? What kind of prophet could he be?"

Jesus compounds the felony by eating and drinking with Levi and all his sinner friends—a "large crowd" of them. In this society, long before McDonald's sold its first hamburger, eating with anyone was a sign of love and belonging. People broke bread with the ones they cared about.

That is Jesus's point: Jesus does eat and drink with sinners: he did it at Levi's home, and he does it now, with us. And he asks us, his disciples, to gather other sinners around the table of his love to eat and drink with them. Though we are unworthy sinners, we are made worthy by the sacrifice of the cross, and we are called to be one with each other and with all the broken world that Jesus has come to love into salvation and eternity.

Prayer

Lord Jesus, my heart can be so cold and so hard. You ate and drank with sinners, but I exclude others from our fellowship because of my petty dislikes. I shun those who have offended me, I gossip and backbite instead of lovingly addressing my issues with others. I avoid those who annoy me and look down on those who are different from me. When the world or the group marginalize someone, I often go along with the crowd because I'm afraid to be different or disliked. Give me courage, Saving Lord, to welcome strangers to fellowship with me. Let my table be a place where sinners of all sorts can come and find acceptance, love, and your saving presence which transforms strangers to friends. I ask this in your name and through the power of the cross. With the Father and the Spirit, you are one God forever and ever. Amen.

Activity

- Invite someone you don't know that well, maybe someone with whom you have a disagreement, to share a meal with you. At that meal, don't argue, just love and be open to the other as that person becomes present to you.
- Focus your prayer today on gratitude: you are one of the sinners the Lord has called to his table!
- Pray the Lord's Prayer slowly and meditatively, and pause at each phrase. Reflect on what it means to forgive, as you have been, by the Father.
- Look into how you can help the marginalized today: check out the Prison Fellowship (prisonfellowship.org), a powerful and effective ministry to prisoners and their families, and see if there is any way you can be part of their great work.

Prayer Journal and Notes

Chapter 2

First Week of Lent

First Sunday of Lent

Scripture Reading

But what does it say? "The word is near you; it is in your mouth and in your heart," that is, the message concerning faith that we proclaim: If you declare with your mouth, "Jesus is Lord," and believe in your heart that God raised him from the dead, you will be saved. For it is with your heart that you believe and are justified, and it is with your mouth that you profess your faith and are saved. As scripture says, "Anyone who believes in him will never be put to shame." For there is no difference between Jew and Gentile—the same Lord is Lord of all and richly blesses all who call on him, for, "Everyone who calls on the name of the Lord will be saved" (Romans 10:8–13).

Reflection

Could salvation be as simple as Paul suggests? Is it just a matter of believing, of faith? Don't I have to *do* something to be saved? No, you don't. It's all grace, which is another way of saying all is a gift, freely given with no strings attached.

Lent is a time to be grateful from the depths of our being for the gift of salvation, something we could never earn or achieve on our own. We make messes all the time. Like Paul, we don't do the good we want to do and find ourselves doing the evil we know we should avoid. We sin, and God chooses to forgive us, love us, and give us life. Only one thing is required: believing in Jesus and giving witness to that belief.

It would be a mistake to think of belief as the assent of the mind to ideas or propositions. For Paul, and for the culture he lived in, belief was best understood as a relationship of trust; to believe in Jesus, in this sense, is to trust in his love, his forgiveness, his power to save and transform our lives. This kind of faith is born of prayer and the word. The more we trust, the more trust grows, and the more we see his love guiding our lives so that we will never be put to shame in the eyes of the Father (and he is the only one whose opinion of us matters).

Then proclaim to those who will listen that Jesus is Lord, and Lord of your life. Let people know that the good you do, your kindness, and your compassion are all rooted in your faith in the one upon whose name you call, the one who saves: Christ Jesus our Lord.

Prayer
We give you thanks, God of Grace, for your amazing love for us. We can do nothing for you, you are all-sufficient in yourself, yet you created us for the pure joy of loving us; and you love us without reservation or exception. We are unworthy, but you make us worthy thought the obedience of your Son, Jesus. We thank you for the gift of life itself; for the beauty of the natural world; for the love of friends and the kindness of strangers. We thank you for your constant care for us, for each breath we take and each step we walk. We thank you, especially, for the gift of saving grace—pure love for us that is made visible in the cross of your Son Jesus.

Activity
- As part of your prayer journal, keep track of all the reasons you have to thank God.

- Give a gift to someone who can do nothing for you in return. Reflect on how, in giving that gift, you are following the example of the God of grace.
- Pray today for atheists and agnostics who do not know the joy of being loved by Love Itself.

Prayer Journal and Notes

Monday of the First Week of Lent

Scripture Reading

"When the Son of man comes in his glory, and all the angels with him, he will sit on his glorious throne. All the nations will be gathered before him, and he will separate the people one from another as a shepherd separates the sheep from the goats. He will put the sheep on his right and the goats on his left.

"Then the King will say to those on his right, 'Come, you who are blessed by my Father; take your inheritance, the kingdom prepared for you since the creation of the world. For I was hungry and you gave me something to eat, I was thirsty and you gave me something to drink, I was a stranger and you invited me in, I needed clothes and you clothed me, I was sick and you looked after me, I was in prison and you came to visit me.'

"Then the righteous will answer him, 'Lord, when did we see you hungry and feed you, or thirsty and give you something to drink? When did we see you a stranger and invite you in, or needing clothes and clothe you? When did we see you sick or in prison and go to visit you?'

"The King will reply, 'Truly I tell you, whatever you did for one of the least of these brothers and sisters of mine, you did for me'" (Matthew 25:31–40).

Reflection

They had no idea! The righteous missed it, and so did the unrighteous on the left. They had no idea that when they were serving (or failing to serve) the least, they were, in fact, serving the Lord. There is no metaphor here; the King does not say, "Whenever you did it for one of these, the least of my brothers and sisters it was *like* doing it for me." Whenever we serve the lowly, the lost, the weak, the unappealing, we are helping our Christ directly, though we may do it unawares.

We have a tremendous opportunity to serve the Lord, and it is revealed right in this passage: when we feed the hungry, we feed the Lord. How often do we see hungry, homeless, struggling people, and just pass them by, thinking of them as bums? It is these very people who reveal to us the other face of God. When we do nothing for them, when we fail to do anything to address their suffering, we are walking past the suffering Christ without lifting a finger to help him.

What can we do, you ask? We can say a prayer, for starters. Then we can give them food, or some concrete assistance. I have a friend who carries single dollar bills just so he can give to the beggars who ask him for help. Some may be scam artists, but some are genuinely in need, and he doesn't want to risk walking past them without helping a little.

Go down the list: where are the needy in our lives, and how can we assist them concretely? Who are the lonely who long for companionship, and how can we extend them some hospitality? Who are the sick, abandoned, or imprisoned, and when can we be present to them?

Prayer

Merciful Father, your son Jesus shows us the way. He was compassionate to the suffering and the marginalized; he befriended those whom the world despised. Open our eyes and our hearts to the pain around us, and give us compassionate and loving spirits. Help us listen to you urging us to do help the weak and support the flagging. Give us the courage and selflessness to be generous to those in need and present to those who are lonely and adrift. We know that whatever we do for the least of our brothers and sisters, we are actually doing for your Son, his love and spirit abide in us and in the suffering of our world. Make us one, Father God, with you and with all of our brothers and sisters. It is that unity which the Lord prayed for on the night before he died when he asked for all of us to be one with each other and one with him, even as he is one with you and you with him. We ask all this in Jesus's name. Amen.

Activity

- If you regularly pass beggars, put some small denomination bills in your pocket and give something, along with a prayer, to whomever asks.
- Give a gift, anonymously, to someone you know who is in need.
- Visit a sick or elderly acquaintance.
- Make the poor a particular focus of your prayer today.
- Check into how you can help a local soup kitchen, food pantry, or feeding ministry.
- If you know someone imprisoned, either in jail or in bondage to some addiction like alcoholism or drugs, reach out in some way: a note, a card, a visit.

Prayer Journal and Notes

Tuesday of the First Week of Lent

Scripture Reading

"And when you pray, do not keep on babbling like pagans, for they think they will be heard because of their many words. Do not be like them, for your Father knows what you need before you ask him.

"This, then, is how you should pray:

"'Our Father in heaven,

hallowed be your name,

your kingdom come,

your will be done,

on earth as it is in heaven.

Give us today our daily bread.

And forgive us our debts,

as we also have forgiven our debtors.

And lead us not into temptation,

but deliver us from the evil one'" (Matthew 6:7–13).

Reflection

In the first words of the prayer, that the Father's name is hallowed: be kept holy. We learn in Revelation 4:8 that, before God's throne in heaven, day and night, the angels sing, "Holy, holy, holy is the Lord God Almighty, who was, and Is, and is to come."

We have trivialized God, and in our effort to make religion "relevant," we can easily forget that we serve the holy God. While he reveals himself to us, he is wholly other. God is awesome, he is majestic, and he is absolutely transcendent. He fills the universe with his might, and before him, the heavens tremble.

Yet, because we have allowed ourselves to become so familiar with our wholly inadequate images of God, we can sometimes take his holy name in vain: the name of the Father or of Jesus the Christ, or of the Holy Spirit. Or we stand by and speak not a word when others use the Lord's name as an expletive. As we pray, we must also commit ourselves to being respectful about the name and the presence of the Holy God.

Prayer

God of majesty, you are holy! Before you we can only cover our face and pray for mercy. We, like Isaiah, are men and women of unclean lips living among a people of unclean lips. Yet we are made worthy of being in your presence by the love and sacrifice of your holy Son. Give us a deep reverence for your name and for your presence within us, and within our world. Help us to stand in awe of you, and to join our voices to the angels who cry out night and day, "Holy, holy, holy is the Lord God Almighty." Keep us, Lord, from taking your name in vain and give us the courage to resist others when they disrespect you or your holy name. We make this prayer in Jesus's name, and through the power for the Spirit, you are one in majesty and in holiness forever and ever. Amen.

Activity

- In prayer, ask God's forgiveness for ever using his name or the name of Jesus as an expletive or in any disrespectful way.
- Read and meditate on Isaiah 6:1-8 and Revelation 4 (the whole chapter).
- Meditate on the holiness of God in the context of Jesus's sacrifice of the cross. The holy God gave up all to show us his unfathomable love for us.

Prayer Journal and Notes

Tuesday of the First Week of Lent

Scripture Reading

"And when you pray, do not keep on babbling like pagans, for they think they will be heard be-cause of their many words. Do not be like them, for your Father knows what you need before you ask him.

"This, then, is how you should pray:
"'Our Father in heaven,
hallowed be your name,
your kingdom come,
your will be done,
on earth as it is in heaven.
Give us today our daily bread.
And forgive us our debts,
as we also have forgiven our debtors.
And lead us not into temptation,
but deliver us from the evil one'" (Matthew 6:7–13).

Reflection

In the first words of the prayer, that the Father's name is hallowed: be kept holy. We learn in Revelation 4:8 that, before God's throne in heaven, day and night, the angels sing, "Holy, holy, holy is the Lord God Almighty, who was, and Is, and is to come."

We have trivialized God, and in our effort to make religion "relevant," we can easily for-get that we serve the holy God. While he reveals himself to us, he is wholly other. God is awe-some, he is majestic, and he is absolutely transcendent. He fills the universe with his might, and before him, the heavens tremble.

Yet, because we have allowed ourselves to become so familiar with our wholly inade-quate images of God, we can sometimes take his holy name in vain: the name of the Father or of Jesus the Christ, or of the Holy Spirit. Or we stand by and speak not a word when others use the Lord's name as an expletive. As we pray, we must also commit ourselves to being respectful about the name and the presence of the Holy God.

Prayer

God of majesty, you are holy! Before you we can only cover our face and pray for mercy. We, like Isaiah, are men and women of unclean lips living among a people of unclean lips. Yet we are made worthy of being in your presence by the love and sacrifice of your holy Son. Give us a deep reverence for your name and for your presence within us, and within our world. Help us to stand in awe of you, and to join our voices to the angels who cry out night and day, "Holy, holy, holy is the Lord God Almighty." Keep us, Lord, from taking your name in vain and give us the courage to resist others when they disrespect you or your holy name. We make this prayer in Je-sus's name, and through the power for the Spirit, you are one in majesty and in holiness forever and ever. Amen.

Activity

- In prayer, ask God's forgiveness for ever using his name or the name of Jesus as an expletive or in any disrespectful way.
- Read and meditate on Isaiah 6:1-8 and Revelation 4 (the whole chapter).
- Meditate on the holiness of God in the context of Jesus's sacrifice of the cross. The holy God gave up all to show us his unfathomable love for us.

Prayer Journal and Notes

Wednesday of the First Week of Lent

Scripture Reading

Then the word of the Lord came to Jonah a second time: "Go to the great city of Nineveh and proclaim to it the message I give you."

Jonah obeyed the word of the Lord and went to Nineveh. Now Nineveh was a very large city; it took three days to go through it. Jonah began by going a day's journey into the city, proclaiming, "Forty more days and Nineveh will be overthrown." The Ninevites believed God. A fast was proclaimed, and all of them, from the greatest to the least, put on sackcloth (Jonah 3:1–5).

Reflection

Nineveh was the capital of the Assyrian Empire. During the time of the Prophets, Assyria took the northern kingdom of Israel into a captivity from which they never returned. They also attacked the southern kingdom and besieged Jerusalem. When God sent Jonah to Nineveh, Jonah did not look forward to the trip, the Ninevites were the enemies of God's people, and the last thing Jonah wanted was to see them spared the Lord's wrath. First, Jonah fled from his mission, but God is not to be deterred by human disobedience. God called to Jonah a second time and commanded him to announce the Lord's pending judgment and call the people there to repentance.

Much to Jonah's chagrin, and God's delight, the Ninevites believed the prophet, repented, and did penance for their sins. God relented and forgave them. Unlike Jonah, who thought provincially, God loves every single human soul he creates, no matter who, no matter where.

Sin, whether in Nineveh or in New York, leads to destruction and death. God does not desire the destruction of sinners. He wants us to repent and live in the light of his love and with the joy that can only be ours when doing his will.

Prayer

Father, you care about all your children wherever and whoever they are. You love your people, and you love those who persecute them. Your great desire is to see sinners turn back to you and find life. You have sent us, like you sent Jonah, to announce your saving message to a sinful world. Give us the courage to proclaim your love through our own loving and compassionate lives. Each day, in small ways and in big ones, through the faithfulness of our lives may your kingdom come and your will be done on earth.

Activity

- Pray for missionaries.
- Make today a fast day, and abstain from meat.

Prayer Journal and Notes

_____

_____

_____

_____

_____

_____

_____

_____

_____

_____

_____

_____

_____

_____

_____

_____

_____

_____

_____

Thursday of the First Week of Lent

Scripture Reading

"Ask and it will be given to you; seek and you will find; knock and the door will be opened to you. For everyone who asks receives; the one who seeks finds; and to the one who knocks, the door will be opened.

"Which of you, if your son asks for bread, will give him a stone? Or if he asks for a fish, will give him a snake? If you, then, though you are evil, know how to give good gifts to your children, how much more will your Father in heaven give good gifts to those who ask him!" (Matthew 7:7–11).

Reflection

The letter of James tells us, "You do not have because you do not ask God" (James 4:2). And when you pray, you do not receive what you ask for because you are asking for selfish reasons.

The Lord wants to give us what we want and need but will never provide us with anything that will harm us. When we ask for the things that the world tells us we want or need, we will be disappointed because God will never give us what will harm us. We may pray for financial wealth so that we can live the high life; God will provide us with spiritual wealth so that we can live a good life. We may pray for health so that we might be strong; God will give us challenges so that we might be compassionate to the weak.

Ask God for his love, for the wisdom that comes from his Spirit, for the courage to live a Christ-like life, and it will be given to you in overflowing measure, and with it, you will receive his providential care. The one who clothes the lilies of the field and feeds the birds of the air will never abandon you (see Matthew 6:25-30).

Prayer

Providential God, we turn to you today in our need. We rely on you for every breath we take; in the morning, it is you who reawakens our souls within us. Provide for us this day: give us food to strengthen our bodies, help us to see your hand touching our lives through the events and interactions of our day. Heal the brokenness of our bodies and spirits even as you make us healers of those whom you send our way for understanding, acceptance, and care. Open our eyes to your wonders all around us so that we might have grateful hearts. We ask this in Jesus's name. Amen.

Activity

- Make a list of all the things you are grateful for and take time to thank God for those blessings.
- In prayer, ask God to give you what you believe you truly need; listen as you pray, and in your prayer journal, write down any inspiration or message that comes to you.
- Look for small ways that you can bless those around you today, and then do them.

Prayer Journal and Notes

Friday of the First Week of Lent

Scripture Reading

"But if a wicked person turns away from all the sins they have committed and keeps all my decrees and does what is just and right, that person will surely live; they will not die. None of the offenses they have committed will be remembered against them. Because of the righteous things they have done, they will live. Do I take any pleasure in the death of the wicked? declares the Sovereign Lord. Rather, am I not pleased when they turn from their ways and live?" (Ezekiel 18:21–23).

Reflection

"Indeed, there is no one on earth who is righteous, no one who does what is right and never sins" (Ecclesiastes 7:20). All of us are sinners, and if we are truthful, from time to time, our sinfulness has made us "wicked." We are wicked when we dehumanize others through our hatred or prejudice; we are wicked when we place our own narrow self-interest above the legitimate interests of others. We are wicked when we harm others, actively or passively, out of spite, jealousy, or fear.

Before the righteous God, though, all sin is an abomination. The great saints of the past have been acutely aware of their sinful unworthiness. St. Patrick prayed: "The Lord opened the understanding of my unbelieving heart so that I should recall my sins." Only when we recall our sins and confront our wickedness can begin the process of repentance.

After the poet-king David's wickedness with Bathsheba, he turned to God: "Have mercy on me, O God, according to your unfailing love; according to your great compassion blot out my transgressions" (Psalm 51:1). His prayer is an honest acknowledgement that he stands a sinner before the Righteous God: "For I know my transgressions, and my sin is always before me" (Psalm 51:3). David knows two things: he stood as a sinner who could be justly condemned; but God is unfailingly merciful, and in his compassion, he wills to blot out the offenses of even those, like David, guilty of terrible things.

The good news for us is that God did not reveal himself to us primarily in his justice but in his love. He made us, and he knows we are weak, and he loves us in spite of our weaknesses and failings. Whoever we are and whatever we've done, he takes no pleasure in our suffering or condemnation. If we but turn to him with a repentant heart, we will live.

Prayer

Forgiving Father, your mercy is unfailing and your compassion boundless. Open our eyes to the full extent of our depravity, so that we may be equally aware of your astounding love for sinners, for us. Help us to acknowledge our sin and keep our transgressions before us always, not so that we might feel guilty and ashamed, but so that we might be grateful for your forgiveness and for the saving death of your Son Jesus, whose blood on the cross has set us free and given us new life. We pray in his saving name. Amen.

Activity

- Before you go to bed, examine your conscience honestly and fearlessly.
- Pray for all sinners who are unaware of their sinfulness because of self-delusion and ask God to give them the grace of health guilt.
- As God has forgiven you so much, forgive someone who needs your forgiveness: forgive him or her fully and with no strings attached.
- Reach out to someone from whom you have become estranged.

Prayer Journal and Notes

Saturday of the First Week of Lent

Scripture Reading

"You have heard that it was said, 'Love your neighbor and hate your enemy.' But I tell you, love your enemies and pray for those who persecute you, that you may be children of your Father in heaven. He causes his sun to rise on the evil and the good, and sends rain on the righteous and the unrighteous. If you love those who love you, what reward will you get? Are not even the tax collectors doing that? And if you greet only your own people, what are you doing more than others? Do not even pagans do that? Be perfect, therefore, as your heavenly Father is perfect" (Matthew 5:43–48).

Reflection

Love your enemies. These words are easy to say after so many years of reading them in the Gospel, but they are hard words to live by. Joseph Campbell calls this teaching of Jesus the "high point of ethical teaching" in all of world history. No ethical teacher has demanded as much of his followers, or given as much of himself.

Real hatred is virulent; it wills and does harm to its objects in personal and vindictive ways. In the face of this kind of hostility, Jesus commands his disciples to love the very ones who despise them.

The Greek word used in the Gospel for love is agape. It means selfless love that looks for no concession or return. Agapic love not an emotion; it is a decision to think and act compassionately and mercifully. We do not "feel" this kind of love, we choose it. When we love agapically, we do not, and often cannot, approve of what our enemy does, but we wish for and pray for his or her best interest; and we do nothing to harm or retaliate against our enemy, and when we can, we help.

Jesus is not merely giving us an ethical maxim here. We must act this way not because it's the nice or right thing to do, but because we are "children of the Most High," who is "kind to the ungrateful and the wicked" (Luke 6:35). When we love our enemies, we are giving witness to the compassionate love of God himself; and when we do that, we make the kingdom of the merciful God visible and present. In our love for "the ungrateful and the wicked" God's promised future of mercy and love breaks into the world. The kingdom comes!

Prayer

Compassionate God, your mercy knows no end, and your kindness fills the whole universe with blessings. Thank you for loving us in our sinfulness and for sending your Son Jesus to save us from sin and death.

Your love is freely given to all. Your rain falls on the just and the unjust; you are kind to the ungrateful and the wicked. Give us the strength to love our enemies and do good to those who have done evil to us. In our love for those who have harmed us show the world your own boundless mercy and love.

Through your Holy Spirit perfect us so that we might be like you, and show the world your loving character. All this we ask in Jesus's name. Amen.

Activity

- Pray for someone who has harmed you in the past.
- Anonymously, do something kind for someone you don't particularly like, and as you do, remind yourself that kindness reflects that of God, who is kind to the wicked and ungrateful.
- In prayer, thank God for his generous kindness to you.

Prayer Journal and Notes

Chapter 3

Second Week of Lent

Second Sunday of Lent

Scripture Reading

[Jesus] took Peter, John, and James with him and went up onto a mountain to pray. As he was praying, the appearance of his face changed, and his clothes became as bright as a flash of lightning. Two men, Moses and Elijah, appeared in glorious splendor, talking with Jesus. They spoke about his departure, which he was about to bring to fulfillment at Jerusalem. Peter and his companions were very sleepy, but when they became fully awake, they saw his glory and the two men standing with him. As the men were leaving Jesus, Peter said to him, "Master, it is good for us to be here. Let us put up three shelters—one for you, one for Moses, and one for Elijah." (He did not know what he was saying.)

While he was speaking, a cloud appeared and covered them, and they were afraid as they entered the cloud. A voice came from the cloud, saying, "This is my Son, whom I have chosen; listen to him" (Luke 9:28–35).

Reflection

In his transfiguration, Jesus's appearance changed. His clothes became dazzling white, like lightning. Lightning is one of the most potent forces in nature. The heat emitted by lightning is almost five times the temperature of the surface of the sun! The energy emitted by lightning is a billion watts per second. In addition to being resplendent, he's standing with Moses and Elijah. This is quite a scene, but God doesn't say, "Look at him." He says, "*Listen* to him."

Listen to him, because while in his transfiguration, Jesus reveals the glorious and glorified Messiah his disciples *want* to know; Jesus's words reveal the Messiah they *need* to know, the one who says: "The Son of man must suffer many things and be rejected by the elders, the chief priests, and the teachers of the law, and he must be killed and on the third day be raised to life" (Luke 9:22).

There is another mountain, besides this mount of where the glory of God will be revealed far more powerfully: Calvary.

The Father wants us to hear Jesus inviting us to pick up our own crosses, to die to ourselves, and to follow him on his way of self-surrender and self-gift. To follow him, we must let go of all selfishness and egoism so we can live from the center of our lives which is the Spirit. Only in the Spirit can we have eternal life, and have it *now*.

Listen to him.

Prayer

Beloved Son of the Father, your glory fills the universe, and in your presence, the angels sing to your glory. Your glory does not rest in clothing that shines like lightning, but in the love you had for the least of our brothers and sisters. You still show your majesty in our world today, if we only had eyes to see. Your glory shines when the suffering are helped, the hungry fed, the marginalized welcomed, and the poor hear Good News. Give us the grace, this day, to see you transfigured in the faces of your little ones. Open our hearts to bring help, hospitality, and good news in your name to everyone we meet. We ask this in your holy name, you live with the Father in the unity of the Holy Spirit, one God forever and ever. Amen.

Activity
- Take a walk today and look for the Glory of God appearing to you in unexpected people or places.
- Pray for the incurably ill asking the Lord to manifest his love for them in their sufferings and praying that they will find a way to unite their sufferings to the sufferings of Christ.
- Spend the day "fasting" from all electronic devices (phones, pads, computers, and TV). Use the time you would have spent on those media for prayer and reading scripture.

Prayer Journal and Notes

Monday of the Second Week of Lent

Scripture Reading

Be merciful, just as your Father is merciful. "Do not judge, and you will not be judged. Do not condemn, and you will not be condemned. Forgive, and you will be forgiven. Give, and it will be given to you. A good measure, pressed down, shaken together and running over, will be poured into your lap. For with the measure you use, it will be measured to you" (Luke 6:36–38).

Reflection

Jesus invites us to reflect the unbounded love of God. He wants us to give of ourselves, in love, to those in need, regardless of who they are. In a world and a nation divided by hatred, Jesus challenges us to create a space in our hearts and lives that transcend all differences; a place where we can love and respect each other as brothers and sisters.

Where are the fissures that divide us? Who is "different" from us? What theories do we fear so much that we despise those who hold them? These are essential questions because once we identify the "outsiders," we must also recognize that God loves them too, and so must we.

Healing starts with empathy and forgiveness: we must accept outsiders, the ones who we disagree with, the ones we dislike and who dislike us. If we perceive that others have done us some harm, forgive from the heart, forgive those trespasses as God forgives us ours. Only with nonjudgmental acceptance and forgiveness can we begin to create a space of love, respect, and caring where we can be present to each other regardless of our differences. In that space, we can begin to heal the soul-wounds that afflict us and our world.

Prayer

Merciful Father, you accept us just as we are: you overlook our faults and forgive our sins when we turn to you with penitent hearts. You ask us to love others as you have loved us. Replace our stony hearts with hearts that love others as you love them. Remove from us our tendency to judge others and to dislike those who disagree with us. Help us to listen to your spirit calling us to care about the outcasts and strangers among us. When we are the objects of hatred or contempt, give us the strength to resist the urge to return evil for evil. Rather inspire us to have forgiving and generous hearts that accept and welcome all, even our enemies. We ask this in Jesus's name, amen.

Activity

- Reflect on the ways you might have judged others and ask the Lord to forgive you and give you a more accepting heart.
- Think of some ways you can be more hospitable and welcoming.
- Invite a new acquaintance from church to join you for coffee; have a neighbor you don't know all that well to your home for dinner.
- Pray for a more welcoming heart.

Prayer Journal and Notes

Tuesday of the Second Week of Lent

Scripture Reading

This is the word that came to Jeremiah from the Lord: "Go down to the potter's house, and there I will give you my message." So I went down to the potter's house, and I saw him working at the wheel. But the pot he was shaping from the clay was marred in his hands; so the potter formed it into another pot, shaping it as seemed best to him.

Then the word of the Lord came to me. He said, "Can I not do with you, Israel, as this potter does?" declares the Lord. "Like clay in the hand of the potter, so are you in my hand, Israel. If at any time I announce that a nation or kingdom is to be uprooted, torn down and destroyed, and if that nation I warned repents of its evil, then I will relent and not inflict on it the disaster I had planned" (Jeremiah 18:1–8).

Reflection

When a potter gets raw clay, he works it with his hands to remove all the impurities that might be in it, impurities that would ultimately ruin the vessel he will make. Before doing anything else, the potter will "wedge" the clay to remove any rocks, other foreign objects, and air pockets.

When the potter begins to work the clay, he may discover that it is centered wrong on the wheel, or he simply may be dissatisfied with his work. No problem—he simply removes the clay, repositions it, and starts over.

Jeremiah's vision of God, the potter, is a profoundly hopeful one. We are the clay in the potter's hands: he works us, shapes us, and molds us to create a vessel of great beauty. Every human being is a work of art, a one-of-a-kind masterpiece. We have been uniquely conceived by the potter, carefully and lovingly created, never again to be repeated.

The challenges and suffering in our life are the potter's way of working the clay into a beautiful shape. When we experience disappointment or loss, it is the Lord's way of removing our impurities and destroying that which destroys us. Through the image of the potter and the clay, God's word invites us to turn to him so that he can make us something beautiful that reflects his own glory.

Prayer

You are the potter, Lord, and we are your clay. Remove our impurities, destroy that within us that is destructive of your will. Make of us what you will. This day we repent of all that keeps our hearts and minds from loving you. Give us minds that embrace your will, hearts that love as you love, and wills that always choose to do what is right and pleasing in your sight. Make us into beautiful vessels that carry and proclaim the good news of your Son Jesus. With you and the Holy Spirit, he lives and reigns forever and ever. Amen.

Activity

- Read chapter 18 in Jeremiah: there is a blessing there, and a profound warning. Meditate on it.
- What are the idols that you may be "worshiping" rather than following the Lord's way?
- What can you do to show the Lord your penitence? Write this in your prayer journal and decide on an action plan.

Prayer Journal and Notes

_____

_____

_____

_____

_____

_____

_____

_____

_____

_____

_____

_____

_____

_____

_____

_____

_____

_____

Wednesday of the Second Week of Lent

Scripture Reading

Now Jesus was going up to Jerusalem. On the way, he took the twelve aside and said to them, "We are going up to Jerusalem, and the Son of man will be delivered over to the chief priests and the teachers of the law. They will condemn him to death and will hand him over to the Gentiles to be mocked and flogged and crucified. On the third day, he will be raised to life!" (Matthew 20:17–19).

Reflection

"The Son of man must suffer many things." The twelve don't want to hear this message, and neither do we. If the truth be told, we would be happy with a messianic sage who teaches beautiful, profound truths and invites us to be wise. We remain uncomfortable with the cross: with the brutality of it: the humiliation, the pain, the suffering, and painful death. Why?

The cross is a theophany, a revelation of the character of God. The cross is part of God's plan: through it, he reveals the depth and height of his love for us all. We can give God nothing in return for our salvation—*nothing*. We have nothing God wants, and everything we do have is a gift from him. Jesus freely chose to disregard his divinity and be born a human being like us. He emptied himself of divinity and was born to a humble woman in a stable in Bethlehem. On the cross, he again emptied himself, giving us everything: his dignity, his body, even his life as his blood poured out. That is how much God loves us. There is no way to calculate it, no way to measure it, and no way to thank God for it.

Every single human being was loved to death on the cross. You were, I was, and all those around us were. Those we agree with were, and those we disagree with were too, including people we like and those we dislike.

Jesus asks us to not just gaze at the cross but to pick up our crosses and follow him. The cross is a theophany: it reveals the character of God. He holds nothing back from us, his beloved. Jesus pours out himself on the cross, having already put off divinity to take upon himself our human nature. We are called to be similarly self-giving. Paul exhorts the Phillipians: "In your relationships with one another, have the same mindset as Christ Jesus: Who, being in the very nature God,,did not consider equality with God something to be used to his own advantage; rather, he made himself nothing by taking the very nature of a servant, being made in human likeness. And being found in appearance as a man, he humbled himself by becoming obedient to death— even death on a cross (Philippians 2:5-8)!

His self-gift must become the pattern for our Christian lives, we, too, must empty ourselves of pride and self-will and become servants to one another. If we would save our lives, Jesus teaches elsewhere, we must lose them by rising above our tendency pride and selfishness. When we pick up our cross, we begin the process of dying to our narrow self-interest and willfulness. Jesus calls us to follow him to Calvary so that "united with him in likeness to his death, so shall we be united to him in the likeness of his resurrection" (Romans 6:5).

Prayer

Lord Jesus, by your cross you have set us free from sin and death. Thank you for the suffering you endured for me, for the burden you took from me and carried to the cross. As you have held nothing back from me, give me the generosity of spirit to hold nothing back from you. Take from me all that is selfish and self-seeking. Place a new heart within me and place your own Holy Spirit within me. Let that Spirit replace my own so that, with Paul, I might truthfully say, "I have been crucified with Christ, and I no longer live, but Christ lives in me. The life I now live in the body, I live by faith in the Son of God, who loved me and gave himself for me" (Galatians 2:20).

Activity

- Fast today to remind your body that your relationship with God in Christ is more important than food. Pray, while you fast, for those who are truly hungry.
- Make a donation to the local food pantry. Don't give money, give food that you buy while thinking of how you can and will bless your hungry neighbors.
- Meditate on your own willfulness, selfishness, and pride. What are some ways you can show repentance? Write them in your journal and work on an action plan for showing repentance in the way you live.

Prayer Journal and Notes

_____

_____

_____

_____

_____

_____

_____

_____

_____

_____

_____

_____

_____

_____

_____

_____

_____

_____

Thursday of the Second Week of Lent

Scripture Reading
This is what the Lord says:
"Cursed is the one who trusts in man,
who draws strength from mere flesh
and whose heart turns away from the Lord.
That person will be like a bush in the wastelands;
they will not see prosperity when it comes.
They will dwell in the parched places of the desert,
in a salt land where no one lives.
"But blessed is the one who trusts in the Lord,
whose confidence is in him" (Jeremiah 17:5–7).

Reflection
According to a Zen story[1], a man was walking in the wilderness when he came across a vicious tiger. As he ran, he came to the edge of a steep cliff. Desperate to escape, he climbed down a vine he found dangling over the cliff. The tiger snorted above him; there was no safe way down. Two mice came out of a hole and began to gnaw on the vine. Just then he noticed a ripe strawberry growing out of the rock near him. He plucked and ate it and thought it was the most delicious thing he had ever eaten.[2]

Dangling on the vine, there is nothing the man can do to save himself. His past, represented by the tiger, crouches to devour him; his future at the bottom of the cliff is certain death; and the strawberry, the pleasures of the present moment, are real but fleeting. The vine represents his security in this life, and it is being eaten away by the troubles of the world. Nothing and no one can save this man; there is only one thing the man can do: he can put his faith in God.

---

[1] Zen stories are parable-like tales used by Zen Buddhist masters to help lead their students to *satori* (enlightenment).

[2] Brennan Manning, *The Ragamuffin Gospel: Good News for the Bedraggled, Beat up, and Burnt Out* (Colorado Springs: Multnomah Books, 2005), Kindle edition, 54.

Jeremiah warns us that whenever we put our trust in "mere flesh," we will be disappointed. Our security does not come from our assets; wealth has no power to save us from the tiger that pursues. In the face of an incurable and terminal illness, all the money in the world is useless. Similarly, if we trust in men—such as politicians who promise us programs to remedy our problems and those of the world—we set ourselves up for bitter disappointment. "Only in God will my soul be at rest," says the psalmist. "He is my rock and salvation" (Psalm 62:1–2).

Prayer

Faithful God, you alone are our rock of safety. We put our trust in you today, trusting in your unfailing love for us. We give over to you all of our worries and concerns, confident that you will care for us as a father caring for his beloved children. When we are tempted to rely on ourselves, or on some human form of security, remind us that there is nothing in this world that can save us; nothing that we can rely on in the face of death. Only you, through your Son Jesus, promise eternal life. Thank you, Father, for all that you have given us, and for the life we have in Jesus's name. Amen.

Activity

- Read and meditate on Psalm 62. What is it that we place our trust in for safety and security?
- How can you rely more intentionally on God's providence? Write about that in your prayer journal.
- What are the cares and worries that are weighing down most heavily on your mind and heart? Spend time putting those cares in the hands of God, trusting in his love for you and in his power.

Prayer Journal and Notes

_____

_____

_____

_____

_____

_____

_____

_____

_____

_____

_____

_____

_____

_____

_____

_____

Friday of the Second Week of Lent

Scripture Reading

Seeing a fig tree by the road, [Jesus] went up to it but found nothing on it except leaves. Then he said to it, "May you never bear fruit again!" Immediately the tree withered.

When the disciples saw this, they were amazed. "How did the fig tree wither so quickly?" they asked.

Jesus replied, "Truly I tell you, if you have faith and do not doubt, not only can you do what was done to the fig tree, but also you can say to this mountain, 'Go, throw yourself into the sea,' and it will be done. If you believe, you will receive whatever you ask for in prayer" (Matthew 21:19–22).

Reflection

Prayer is powerful, and Jesus expects his disciples to be powerful in prayer. The disciples were amazed by Jesus's command over the forces of nature, whether it was cursing the barren fig tree or calming the storms on the Sea of Galilee. But Jesus tells them that they too can exercise power through faith-filled prayer.

There are two challenges here. First, and most importantly, we need to come to God with faith. Faith, here, is not the same as mere belief; it is confidence rooted in relationship. Jesus has power in prayer because of his intimate relationship with the Father. When he promises that we too can be powerful in prayer, he makes it clear that a prerequisite of that power is that we also must have an intimate relationship with the Father through the Son.

The second challenge is to have boldness in prayer. For the mountain to throw itself into the sea, we must first have the courage to ask for it to do so. What are the mountains that we would like the Lord to cast into the deepest sea? Perhaps they are the mountains of our sin or guilt: maybe it is the mountain of memories we have of long years of hurt and abuse. Whatever our mountains are, when we are in Christ, we have the power to ask God to cast them through the sea.

Prayer

Father God, you hear the prayers of your beloved children and answer them in love. Even when we ask you for wonders beyond our wildest dreams, when we have a loving and intimate relationship with you through your Son Jesus, you will hear and answer our prayer with power. Give us the gift of faith, loving Father; keep us close to you so that every moment of our lives we are in union with you and with your will. We long to walk with you as our Father and friend, and in Jesus, we do just that. Knowing your love, make us bold in prayer, asking that your wonders might unfold in our lives through healing and forgiveness. Cast the mountains of our sin, guilt, shame, and discouragement into the deepest sea so that we can know the warmth and tenderness of your love for us. Heal our nation and our world of its sinfulness and make of your creation, as you promised, a new heaven and a new earth. We ask all this in Jesus's name. Amen.

Activity

- Meditate on the mountains in your life that you would like the Lord to cast into the sea, and write about that in your prayer journal.
- Pray for a deeper and more loving relationship with the Father through Christ the Son. What can you do to respond to the grace that God is flooding in your life? Write what comes to you in your prayer journal.
- Pray for healing the hatred and mistrust in our nation and in our world.

Prayer Journal and Notes

Saturday of the Second Week of Lent

Scripture Reading

Who is a God like you,
who pardons sin and forgives the transgression
of the remnant of his inheritance?
You do not stay angry forever.
but delight to show mercy.
You will again have compassion on us;
you will tread our sins underfoot
and hurl all our iniquities into the depths of the sea.
You will be faithful to Jacob,
and show love to Abraham,
as you pledged on oath to our ancestors
in days long ago (Micah 7:18–20).

Reflection

God is faithful to his promises, and his promise to us is that he loves us and forgives us with no strings attached. We are sinners, and we need to acknowledge that fact. We are constantly choosing our will over God's, and whenever we do that we choose death over life, suffering over joy. Only God's ways are perfect, and only when we follow the path he charts for our lives can we experience the peace that surpasses all understanding, the peace that our Jewish brothers and sisters call shalom.

Sinful as we are, God continually reaches out to us, promising to forgive us for whatever wrong we do, promising to give us a fresh start. In his first letter, John urges us to set our hearts at rest in God's presence even as we feel the weight of our sins burdening our hearts because God is greater than our hearts. In him there is no condemnation, just pure grace. And we cooperate with that grace by living lives of love and forgiveness, by striving, however imperfectly, to believe in the name of Jesus, and to love one another. When we strive to do this, we are in God, and he is in us.

God, the prophet Micah reminds us, delights in mercy and has boundless compassion for us in our sinfulness. So, Micah invites, turn back to the one who has never turned away from you. What we perceive to be his anger is actually the anger within us when we live apart from his will; what we perceive to be his punishment is, in reality, the natural consequences of life lived against the will of God.

The promise of Lent is forgiveness: God longs to hurl our sin into the depths of the sea, if only we let him.

Prayer

Forgiving Lord, we turn to you in our need and trust in your love for us. We could never deserve your compassion, but you freely give us grace upon grace: gift upon gift. Every day you renew our life within us as you wake us from sleep. Every day you come to us in thousands of ways that we often fail to see or understand. Still, you never give up on us. Hurl all our wickedness and injustice into the depths of the sea, and in its place give us eyes that see as you see, and a heart that loves as you love. Help us to delight in your will and walk in your ways always. We ask this in Jesus' name, and through the power of the Spirit, they are one God with you forever and ever, amen.

Activity

- In your prayer journal, write the sins and transgressions you'd like the Lord to "hurl into the depths of the sea." Pray with thanksgiving that, even as you are asking, God is hurling.
- What are the ways God is showing you his lovingkindness today? Reflect on them and write your reflection in your prayer journal.
- Pray for the repentance of sinners; pray for the conversion of one person you know who does not know Christ yet. Keep this person in prayer for the rest of Lent.

Prayer Journal and Notes

Chapter 4

Third Week of Lent

Third Sunday of Lent

Scripture Reading

Seek the Lord while he may be found;
call on him while he is near.
Let the wicked forsake their ways
and the unrighteous their thoughts.
Let them turn to the Lord, and he will have mercy on them,
and to our God, for he will freely pardon (Isaiah 55:6–7).

Reflection

Celtic mystics speak of the "thin places," where the veil separating earth and heaven seem particularly "thin," where we begin to experience the earth as being "crammed with heaven." In a thin place we become aware of the nearness of God; his power and presence permeate the atmosphere, though we might now be able to explain precisely how or why we are aware of this. In thin places, the world is revealed to itself as dwelling in the presence and power of God, something of which we become forgetful as we go about our ordinary lives in the noise, haste, and hurry of our workaday lives.

Lent invites us into a thin place, where the presence of the Lord can be more readily perceived and understood. Throughout the centuries, for more than two millennia, Christians have made the forty days before Easter a sacred time devoted to prayer, fasting, and penance. Each Lent we are invited to go into the wilderness with the Lord. As he fasted and prayed, so must we if we are to find the nearness of God in this holy season.

Lent is a time to seek the one who is seeking us, to call upon him knowing he is near. In this sacred time and space, we are invited to reflect on our ways and forsake any wickedness and unrighteousness. It is not popular to talk about sin and wicked behavior, but to be right with God we must also be honest with ourselves. Lent is a time to know who we are and to know what we must change to be more aligned with the will of the Father.

Every Lent, heaven draws closer to earth. In the Lord's nearness, we can seek and find God's saving love and experience his freely given pardon and mercy. Quoting Isaiah, Paul writes: "In the time of my favor I heard you, and in the day of salvation I helped you." Paul goes on: "I tell you, now is the time of God's favor; now is the day of salvation" (2 Corinthians 6:2).

Seek the Lord!

Prayer

Draw near, O Lord our God. Make this Lent, for us, a thin place where we can feel your closeness and know your saving power. In the light of your holiness, we see and understand our complete unworthiness. We stand as beggars before you, yet you draw us into your presence and shower us with love and blessings. Make us aware of your nearness to us this Lent. Give us the grace to take advantage of your closeness to grow in goodness and in righteousness. Transform us, Lord, mold us into our most essential selves: the people you created us to be. We ask this in Jesus' name, he is the one who tears the veil separating earth and heaven forever. He lives with you, yet his Spirit remains with us until the end of the ages. Amen.

Activity

In your prayer journal, reflect on your "thin places." Where is it that you feel the presence of God most powerfully in your life? If you can, spend some time there today.

Meditate on the nearness of God in this holy season of Lent. Write about your thoughts in your prayer journal.

Prayer Journal and Notes

_____

_____

_____

_____

_____

_____

_____

_____

_____

_____

_____

_____

_____

_____

_____

_____

_____

Monday of the Third Week of Lent

Scripture Reading

He called a little child to him and placed the child among them. And he said: "Truly I tell you, unless you change and become like little children, you will never enter the kingdom of heaven. Therefore, whoever takes the lowly position of this child is the greatest in the kingdom of heaven. And whoever welcomes one such child in my name welcomes me (Matthew 18:2–5).

Reflection

In our culture, we have romanticized children and childhood, but it was not so in Jesus's day. Then, children were neither valued nor favored: children had no standing at all; they didn't matter and were even ridiculed and scorned. When Jesus tells his disciples that they must become like little children, he is telling them that they must become one with the marginalized and unimportant. "The little child who is the image of the kingdom is a symbol of those who have the lowest place in society: the poor, the oppressed, the beggars, the prostitutes, and tax collectors—the people whom Jesus often called the "little ones."[3]

While the world tells us to become great, the Lord tells us that we must be one with the poor, the despised, the humble. This isn't merely a "nice" thing to do, it is an essential thing to do: our salvation depends on us.

It is easy for Christians to make the same mistake the Pharisees made: in our striving to follow Christ and live godly lives, we can easily become proud ("Oh, what a good boy [or girl] am I"). It is a short hop from this kind of pride to becoming judgmental ("I'm better than that one over there"). The Lord is clear that this is not what he expects of us. He expects us to be in touch with our brokenness, and to know that, like children, we depend on our

---

[3] Mannning, Ragamuffin Gospel, 51.

Father for everything, for life itself. Without God's grace, we are nothing.

When Jesus tells us to become like little children, he is instructing us to acknowledge that we are one with the poor, the suffering, the broken, and the lost. That means we must accept those whom others reject; we must use our resources to help those less fortunate than ourselves; we must extend hospitality to those others would exclude as strangers or "aliens."

Remember, when we welcome the little ones in Christ's name, we welcome Jesus himself, and when we welcome him, we welcome the Father who sent him.

Prayer

Make us like little children, Lord. We reject all pretense and recognize that we are as nothing before you, yet you love us. And you love those others, too. The ones whom the world denies. Give us the wisdom and courage to accept all your children. Help us to find a place in our hearts for the poor, the misunderstood, the lonely, the frightened children whom you send across our path. Help us to love them, in your name, until they are whole. Finally, Father, give us humble and contrite spirits, protect us, always, from the deadly sin of pride. We ask all this in Jesus's name. Amen.

Activity

- What can you do to become more like a little child? Answer this in your prayer journal as if your life depends on it, because it does!
- How can you actively love the little ones? What can you *do* (in a concrete, practical way) to reach out to the least of Jesus's brothers and sisters? Now do it.

Prayer Journal and Notes

Tuesday of the Third Week of Lent

Scripture Reading

"What do you think? If a man owns a hundred sheep, and one of them wanders away, will he not leave the ninety-nine on the hills and go to look for the one that wandered off? And if he finds it, truly I tell you, he is happier about that one sheep than about the ninety-nine that did not wander off. In the same way your Father in heaven is not willing that any of these little ones should perish (Matthew 18:12–14).

Reflection

The parable of the lost sheep will never end up as a case study at the Harvard Business School, or any other business school, for that matter. What Jesus proposes in the parable makes no human sense. What sheep owner in his right mind would risk 99 percent of his flock to find one lost sheep? He would cut his losses, take a business deduction on his taxes, and chalk the loss of sheep to the cost of doing business.

Jesus is not giving a lesson in sheepherding here; this is a parable about the reckless love of God. Though our ears have grown used to hearing this parable and others like it, the Lord's original hearers would have been scratching their heads and wondering what Jesus's story was all about. What was he teaching about God, and why should it matter to us?

The Father is not willing to lose a single sheep. This is very good news for those of us who are prone to wander from the fold from time to time. When we wander, we are not left alone to fend for ourselves. The Good Shepherd will be searching for us wherever we roam. We can feel lost from time to time, we may even feel lost for extended periods; whether we know it or not, though, we are not alone. The shepherd seeks us out and is with us even though we're unaware. He never leaves us, never gives up on us, never just "cuts his losses" and cuts us loose.

Hear the joy Jesus speaks about when one of the lost comes

home. God is happier than he would be over the sheep that didn't wander. There's only one problem—all of us "sheep" wander, get lost, and are precious in the eyes of the Good Shepherd.

Prayer

Lord Jesus, you are the Good Shepherd. You know us and call us by name. When we are lost, you seek us out. When we are in trouble, you rescue us; when we think we are alone and abandoned, you are still with us; you never leave us. Help us to know your love and return to you and to our Father's house. Thank you for your faithful love and tender care for us. As you have loved us, so may we love each other; we are all the sheep of your pasture. We pray for the day when all will be united with us, and there will be one fold and one Good Shepherd of the sheep. You are Lord with the Father in the unity of the Holy Spirit, one God forever and ever. Amen.

Activity

- Reflect on the fact that "the Father in heaven is not willing that any one of these little ones shall perish" (Matthew 18:14). What does that mean about the grace of God and the love he has for each of us? Write about this in your prayer journal.
- How can you help the Good Shepherd in his mission? Ask the Lord to show how you can function as his assistant shepherd (sheepdog?). Write about your thoughts in your prayer journal, and decide on action steps.

Prayer Journal and Notes

Wednesday of the Third Week of Lent

Scripture Reading

"Do not think that I have come to abolish the Law or the Prophets;
I have not come to abolish them but to fulfill them. For truly I tell
you, until heaven and earth disappear, not the smallest letter, not
the least stroke of a pen, will by any means disappear from the Law
until everything is accomplished. Therefore, anyone who sets aside
one of the least of these commands and teaches others accordingly
will be called least in the kingdom of heaven, but whoever practices
and teaches these commands will be called great in the kingdom of
heaven (Matthew 5:17–19).

Reflection

The Law of God is his love and compassion in action. The Torah is
God's great gift, not only to the Jewish people but to the entire
world. While there are 613 laws of varying importance in the Torah,
those laws can be boiled down to their essence. The prophet Micah
summarized the Law in this way: "What does the Lord require of
you? To act justly and to love mercy and to walk humbly with your
God" (Micah 6:8). The rabbi and Jewish sage Hillel the Elder was
once asked to sum up the entire Torah while standing on one foot.
He answered: "That which is distasteful to you do not do unto
another ... all the rest is commentary. Go and learn."[4]

But Jesus gives us the most beautiful and complete summary of
the Law. When a teacher of the Law asked Jesus which commandment
of the Law was the greatest, the Lord answered, "Love." Love the
Lord your God with everything in you (your whole heart, mind, and
soul), and love all others as you love yourself. The Torah and the
prophets both rest their teachings on these commandments of love.

This Law will never be abolished, and it applies to everything we
do, think, and say. If you think unloving thoughts, change the way
you're thinking; if you do unloving acts, change what you're doing;

---

[4] Hillel, Babylonian Talmud, *Shabbat* 31.

if you say unloving things, speak rather of love. Our thoughts have power; we do nothing that hasn't started as a thought. So, we must take control of our thoughts lest they take control of us. We must choose love in every way possible, thereby living fully into the Law that will never be done away with.

Prayer

Loving Lord, your Law of love invites us to live as you yourself live. As we love you with all of our being, and as we love our others as we love ourselves, we give witness to your own love, and we display what it is like to live in your kingdom. Thank you for loving us so completely. In your great love for us you accepted death on the cross. You died as you lived, loving even your enemies and forgiving those who tormented you. Rejected by the world on the cross, your Father embraced your obedience and, in your resurrection, He shows the entire universe that love leads to life that never ends. We ask for the courage to live lives of love and compassion as your disciples. We ask this in your holy name. Amen.

Activity

- Surprise someone you know and love with a present. Make it yourself, or buy it after careful, loving thought.
- Meditate on how you can express your love for God in some tangible way. Write your thoughts in your prayer journal and then do something special for God.
- Pray for the Jewish people, our elder brothers and sisters in faith. Pray for the peace of Jerusalem and for peace in the entire state of Israel.

Prayer Journal and Notes

Thursday of the Third Week of Lent

Scripture Reading

This is what the Lord Almighty, the God of Israel, says: Reform your ways and your actions, and I will let you live in this place. Do not trust in deceptive words and say, "This is the temple of the Lord, the temple of the Lord, the temple of the Lord!" If you really change your ways and your actions and deal with each other justly, if you do not oppress the foreigner, the fatherless or the widow and do not shed innocent blood in this place, and if you do not follow other gods to your own harm, then I will let you live in this place, in the land I gave your ancestors forever and ever (Jeremiah 7:3–7).

Reflection

"Actions speak louder than words." We all probably learned that maxim as children, and here, through the prophet Jeremiah, we have God telling his people in Israel, and by extension, us, that he is not impressed with empty gestures.

A quick look at recent events will remind us that some of the most sacred institutions, and the loftiest of churchmen, have been revealed to be tarnished. Televangelists lead double lives and waste the money sent to them by faithful, and often poor, listeners. High-ranking bishops are unmasked as sexual predators preying on the weak and vulnerable. Politicians claiming to be impeccably honest prove to be corrupt.

The Lord does not judge on appearances, nor is he impressed by reputation. He sees our hearts and knows who we are. It is not enough to go to the temple or cry out, "Lord, Lord!" He expects us to live like sons and daughters of the just and loving God.

What the Lord wants is justice; he wants us to be fair to others and to have integrity when dealing with others. He wants us to be welcoming and hospitable, not only to our own but even to strangers. That is how he is. He loves all, regardless of who they are or how they behave. He expects us to be kind and loving to the least among us: the marginalized, the mentally or physically challenged, the poor, the ignorant.

Above all, the Lord expects us to put him first. If we put anything in his place, if we want to please anyone more than we want to please him, then we are honoring the false gods of this world, and they will always disappoint.

As he called to Israel, so he invites us to repent, live lives of justice and love, and be faithful to the Faithful God who made us.

Prayer

Faithful God, we repent of our sinful thoughts and sinful actions. We have not always loved others as you ask us to love them. We have placed our own interests first and acted selfishly and unjustly. When lonely and marginalized people come into our lives, we ignore them rather than offer them hospitality. We rationalize our own corruption and pretend to serve you when we are only serving ourselves. Worst of all, Lord God, we have put the things of this world—wealth, power, popularity, and fame—in your place and worshiped in their temple rather than in yours. We turn back to you now, Lord, repenting of our sinful ways. And we trust that you forgive us fully and bid us live. For all this we give you thanks in Jesus's name. Amen.

Activity

- Think of some ways that you can show hospitality to someone new to your church, and then reach out.
- Reflect on your false gods. What interests and desires do you put in God's place? Write about this in your prayer journal, and write some of the changes you will make in the way you live.
- What are some ways that you can be more just? Remember, justice is active, so we need to look for ways to benefit the Lord's little ones.

Prayer Journal and Notes

Friday of the Third Week of Lent

Scripture Reading

One of the teachers of the Law came and heard them debating. Noticing that Jesus had given them a good answer, he asked him, "Of all the commandments, which is the most important?"

"The most important one," answered Jesus, "is this: 'Hear, O Israel: The Lord our God, the Lord is one. Love the Lord your God with all your heart and with all your soul and with all your mind and with all your strength.' The second is this: 'Love your neighbor as yourself.' There is no commandment greater than these" (Mark 12:28–31).

Reflection

The Lord quotes the *Sh'ma*, the prayer that pious Jews recite at least twice a day: "*Sh'ma Yisrael Adonai Eloheinu Adonai echad*" ("Hear, O Israel, the Lord your God is Lord alone") (Deuteronomy 6:4). The prayer goes on: "love the Lord your God with all your heart, and with all your soul, and with all your strength." In answering the teacher of the Law with these words, Jesus is going to the heart of the Jewish tradition: to the heart of the Law.

Let's look at the first two words of the prayer: The word *sh'ma* means "hear!" We are to listen to the commandments of the Lord with the ears of our heart. Most of us spend so much time talking, so much time surrounding ourselves with noise, that we're not very good listeners. We are almost addicted to noise: many of us can't abide silence for a moment. I know people (and was once one of them) who come home and immediately turn on the television or radio just to have sound in the house. The sh'ma asks us to listen for the voice of God in our lives, and to do that we have to find a quiet space, or make one, in our world.

Next, we have Yisrael. Israel is the name of a nation, but first it was the name the Lord gave to the patriarch Jacob after he wrestled all night with a mysterious stranger. At daybreak, the stranger told Jacob: "Your name will no longer be Jacob but Israel, because you have struggled with God and with humans and have overcome" (Genesis 32:28).

Like Israel the patriarch, we must become "God-wrestlers." The Lord wants us to wrestle with our faith so that it deepens and changes over time, as every good relationship must. Couples must struggle with their love over time or see that love die; friends either deepen their friendship or grow apart. God wants us to love him actively, with struggling, questioning hearts. He never wants us to accept easy, pat answers. He wants us to honestly examine our faith, struggle with him and with his ways, and even become comfortable with the mystery that lies at the heart of it all. Love embraces mystery—it is only with the heart that we can enter into a relationship, with God or anyone, for that matter. Our hearts can love what our minds can never fathom.

Prayer

Mysterious God, you are the mystery that lies at the heart of the universe. We stand before you in awe. Your ways are as far away from us as the east is from the west. Your plans are impossible for us to fathom. So, we come to you with trust, all that we can know of you, you have revealed to us in the life, teaching, death, and resurrection of your Son, he is the image of your majesty and love. In his cross, we know your love, and in his resurrection, we know your power. Open our hears so that we can listen to you when you speak to us: in prayer, in your word, in the events of our lives or the history of our world. When we do not understand you, give us the faithful love that allows us to struggle with you and question you, while never rejecting you or turning from you. Give us hearts that lovingly embrace your mystery even as we strive to understand your actions in our world. This we ask in the name of Jesus your Son, amen.

Activity

- Spend at least half an hour in quiet meditation.

- Go on a "device fast": turn off all your electronic devices so that you can experience a quiet, restful space in which the voice of God might be more easily heard. Write in your prayer journal about this fast and what it was like for you.
- It's Friday: fast and abstain from meat with your physician's approval.

Prayer Journal and Notes

Saturday of the Third Week of Lent

Scripture Reading

"Come, let us return to the Lord.
He has torn us to pieces.
but he will heal us;
he has injured us
but he will bind up our wounds.
After two days he will revive us;
on the third day he will restore us,
that we may live in his presence.
Let us acknowledge the Lord;
let us press on to acknowledge him.
As surely as the sun rises,
he will appear;
he will come to us like the winter rains,
like the spring rains that water the earth" (Hosea 6:1–3).

Reflection

The prophets often announce the Lord's judgment against Israel, but judgment is never their last word. The Lord judges his sinful people because he is just; he punishes them because sin bears within it its own punishment, but his last word is always forgiveness.

All prophetic utterance in the Hebrew Bible reveals the tenderness of God. He longs to bind the wounds caused by our sin and make us whole. His anger lasts but a moment, but his lovingkindness is eternal.

What is true of sinful Israel was lived out in the passion, death, and resurrection of the Messiah. He alone is sinless, but on Calvary, he stands in the place of us sinners. He carries our burdens, suffers for our sins, and is injured because of our transgressions. He died for us and was buried before sunset on that first Good Friday night. Death seemed to have a victory over the light of the world.

Death's victory was only an illusion, though. The cross was the world's "no" to the Gospel of Grace, which Jesus came to proclaim.

The resurrection on the third day was the Father's "yes" to his son and the vindication of his message. Jesus, the Messiah, who rose on the third day, guarantees the word of life he proclaims. God does not condemn the world, he saves it through the suffering, death, and resurrection of his Son.

When we acknowledge Jesus as Lord of our lives, when we say yes to him and his word, and when we live in the kingdom, which he proclaimed to be present *now*, we have life in his name. In Christ we are born again, we are radically new, and we become what we were created to be: sons and daughters of God, "Children not born of natural descent nor of human decision ... but born of God" (John 1:13).

Prayer

Lord our God, your love for us is incomprehensible to our mortal minds. We wander and sin, we lose our way regularly, but you never cease to love us. Our sins bear our punishment within them; when we are apart from your will, we are out of contact with life itself. We try to find happiness apart from you but can never succeed, in you alone can we find joy and peace. We turn back to you, today, with all our heart, and what we are unable to do to return to you, Father God, please you do within us. We turn to you and give you our minds: let our every thought be rooted in you. We give you our hearts: may we love all that you love and despise only the evil that is hateful in your eyes. We give you our souls, let your Holy Spirit be the center of our souls. We ask all this in the name of the One who died for us and now is risen. With you and the Holy Spirit, he is Lord forever and ever. Amen.

Activity

- In prayer, reaffirm your commitment to making Jesus the Lord and Savior of your life. What are some of the ways you can give witness to this reality? Write about that in your prayer journal.

- In what ways has the Lord appeared in your life? Meditate on that question and then write what comes to you in your prayer journal.
- Begin a daily list of everything you are grateful for, and use it to give thanks to God.

Prayer Journal and Notes

Chapter 5

Fourth Week of Lent

Fourth Sunday of Lent

Scripture Reading

Blessed is the one
whose transgressions are forgiven,
whose sins are covered.
Blessed is the one
whose sin the Lord does not count against them
and in whose Spirit is no deceit.
When I kept silent,
my bones wasted away
through my groaning all day long.
For day and night,
your hand was heavy on me;
my strength was sapped
as in the heat of summer.
Then I acknowledged my sin to you
and did not cover up my iniquity.
I said, "I will confess
my transgressions to the Lord."
And you forgave
the guilt of my sin (Psalm 32:1–5).

Reflection

"Blessed is the one … in whose spirit is no deceit!"

The truth is, every one of us are sinners. Sin, in every form, is wandering from obedience to the will of the Creator. His will is the only path that leads to life, joy, peace, and happiness. When we choose our will over his, we are really choosing death rather than life. When we are selfish, we harm the very self we seek to satisfy. Simply put, sin is death. When we sin, we choose to waste the precious gift of time. A moment of sin is a moment when we reject the better plan for our lives that God has offered us. Once wasted, that moment can never come back to us; it is gone forever. No power on earth and no power of our own can redeem those many moments lost to sin and self-seeking.

There is hope, though. What we can't do, God can. When we acknowledge our sinfulness and take it to God, he can forgive our transgressions and cover our sins.

Embedded in this psalm is the Hebrew concept of repentance. The Hebrew word for repentance is *teshuva*, which means to "turn" or "return." Repentance, in this sense, is to turn away from sin and to return to living in obedience to God. Teshuva is more than feeling sorry for sin. To repent, in this sense, we must do an honest examination of our lives: before we repent, we must know we are sinners and acknowledge our sin to God and to ourselves. How have we broken faith with God or with others? Who have we betrayed; how have we fallen short; in what ways have we lost our integrity or strayed morally? This inner work is a necessary starting point for repentance.

When people discover their flaws, they often look for someone to blame, but teshuva requires us to be personally accountable. We are responsible for sinfulness, no one else. In the words of Pogo: "We have met the enemy, and he is us." [5]

Finally, teshuva requires that we look for ways to make amends for the damage our sin has caused. Repentance, thus understood,

---

[5] Walt Kelly, Pogo daily comic strip, April 22, 1971 (Earth Day).

holds out the possibility that we can be fully reconciled to God and to our communities; that we can change our lives; and that even our flaws can be sanctified. There is no brokenness that God cannot transform into something beautiful when we trustingly place it before him. We can do none of this by ourselves, we need God's help; we need a savior.

Rabbi Eleazar ben Hyrcanus, a first-century Jewish sage, taught his students that they should repent the day before their death. His students objected: "How, teacher, can we know the day of our death?" "Then you must repent today," the rabbi taught them.

There will be a time when there is no time left, but if we are still breathing, there is hope.[6]

Prayer

Forgiving God, you long to heal us and make us whole. You are always with us, and your compassion envelops us. We are sinners; we cannot stand on our own righteousness, nor can we save ourselves. We lack the courage and the honesty to confront our own sinfulness and evil; instead, we pretend that we are good and worthy when nothing could be further from the truth. Until we acknowledge iniquity and confess our sin, we will suffer the agony of being apart from you: our spirits will waste away for lack of the healing warmth of your Spirit. And so, Father, we acknowledge our need for your love and forgiveness. We are sinners, and we have done evil in your sight. We have wandered from the path you call us to walk even though it alone is the path to the fullness of life in your presence. Forgive us, Lord, blot out our offenses, and cover our guilt in the saving blood of your Son Jesus. Even though he was without sin, he chose to be near sin to save us and restore us to you. It is in his name we pray. Amen.

---

[6] Joe Laur, "Returning to Our Best Selves" (blog post), retrieved on March 1, 2016, from https://todaysrabbi.wordpress.com/tag/repentance/.

Activity

- Make an inventory of your moral and spiritual life. What sins have you failed to acknowledge and bring to the Lord for forgiveness?
- Pray for the grace of self-understanding.
- Ask the Lord to forgive your sins, remembered and unremembered.
- Give thanks for God's mercy.
- Forgive someone who needs you to wipe some slate clean. Don't make a big deal about it, just quietly do it.
- If necessary, make some gesture to let another know you care about him or her: a phone call, a letter, a small gift. Be creative.

Prayer Journal and Notes

Monday of the Fourth Week of Lent

Scripture Reading

"See, I will create
new heavens and a new earth.
The former things will not be remembered,
nor will they come to mind.
But be glad and rejoice forever
in what I will create,
for I will create Jerusalem to be a delight
and its people a joy.
I will rejoice over Jerusalem
and take delight in my people;
the sound of weeping and of crying
will be heard in it no more" (Isaiah 65:17–19).

Reflection

Hope is the heart of all prophetic utterance. God has a beautiful plan for his creation, which, though marred by sin, has not destroyed. While God punishes evil brought into the world by sin, he intends to restore all creation to his original plan. God created a world to be perfectly aligned with is will, a place of peace and harmony, where the lion and the lamb could lie together because there would be no more harm, no more destruction, no more suffering; instead, the "the earth would be filled with the knowledge of the Lord" (Isaiah 11:9).

God will redeem everything he created. What you see in our world: what you love and cherish, what you enjoy and love, will never be lost. Instead, God has planned to restore everything in the "new heaven and a new earth." This is the place where all tears will be wiped away; every broken heart will be fully restored. Having triumphed on Calvary, God's love will infuse all things. Our humanity will again reflect the God in whose image we have been created.

While God's kingdom is his work, he chooses us to be his helpers.

We are in the process of creating, with the Father, the new heaven and earth that will be finally established when the Lord comes again, in Glory. Get to work!

Prayer

Creator God, we thank you for everything we have and everything we are. You created the beauty of nature, and you give us joy through all things. You have given us hearts to love with and minds open to the incredible beauty all around us. You made nothing in vain, and nothing you bring into existence is lost; all things come from you, and all will return to you. In you, we live and move and have our being. You promise that nothing is ever lost; what is sown here in tears we will reap rejoicing. We wait for the new heaven and the new earth you promised. In that place there will be no weeping, or loss, or pain; all that we perceive to have been lost in this life we live now will be restored. And so we pray for your kingdom to come. We long for the day when your son will return to establish your kingdom in its fullness. Come, Lord Jesus. Amen.

Activity

- Take a walk and consciously look for the beauty that surrounds you and that you so often overlook. Write about this experience in your prayer journal.
- Write a thank you note to someone you appreciate. Tell that person how much he or she means to you.
- In your prayer journal, write a thank you note to God.

Prayer Journal and Notes

_____

_____

_____

_____

_____

_____

_____

_____

_____

_____

_____

_____

_____

_____

_____

_____

_____

_____

Tuesday of the Fourth Week of Lent

Scripture Reading
Wash and make yourselves clean.
Take your evil deeds out of my sight;
stop doing wrong.
Learn to do right; seek justice.
Defend the oppressed.
Take up the cause of the fatherless;
plead the case of the widow (Isaiah 1:16–17).

Reflection
God cherishes the most vulnerable among us. Through the prophets, the Lord reminds his people—including us—that the most important way we can express our love for and faithfulness to God is by the way we care for the poor, the suffering, the weak, the broken, and the lost. This, he tells us, is what he wants more than our prayers or our sacrifices. Paraphrasing the prophet Micah, the Lord asks us to love justice, love tenderly, and walk humbly with our God. The good news in this message is that, if we see ourselves honestly, we are beggars before the Lord. We have nothing that hasn't been given to us; we deserve none of the blessings we have received. All is a gift; all is grace.

When we become aware of how much God loves us in our poverty when we accept that nothing is truly ours, then how can we deny those who struggle and suffer around us. Who are the oppressed in our world? The word oppression means to crush or heavily burden: kids who are bullied are oppressed; people perceived to be "odd" are oppressed; those marginalized because of their unpopular views are oppressed.

Whoever the oppressed are, as Christians, we must defend them. That may make us unpopular too, but our role is clear: the oppressed, weak, and vulnerable are our responsibility. God loves them and cares for them through us. We cannot be part of the oppressive crowd; we must stand against that crowd and be a voice for the voiceless.

Prayer

Father of all justice, give us the courage to give voice to your passion for the weak and helpless. You are a God of boundless compassion. Your love fills our lives with hope and care. You care for the vulnerable, and shelter your little ones in your arms. You ask us to give voice to the silent cry of the poor. When we see oppression, show us how to oppose it. Fill us with your courageous spirit and make us a sword in your hand, so that we can execute your commands and protect the ones you send us for help and safety. We ask this through the One whose courage on the cross gives us safe shelter; he is Lord with you forever and ever. Amen.

Activity

- Reflect on who, in your life, is vulnerable and in need of your help. Write about it in your prayer journal. What concrete things can you do to help them?
- Pray for the world's oppressed; especially pray for Christians throughout the world who are suffering because of their faith.
- Consider joining a group like Voice of the Martyrs (www. persecution.com).

Prayer Journal and Notes

Wednesday of the Fourth Week of Lent

Scripture Reading

"Very truly I tell you, the Son can do nothing by himself; he can do only what he sees his Father doing, because whatever the Father does the Son also does. For the Father loves the Son and shows him all he does. Yes, and he will show him even greater works than these so that you will be amazed. For just as the Father raises the dead and gives them life, even so, the Son gives life to whom he is pleased to give it. Moreover, the Father judges no one, but has entrusted all judgment to the Son, that all may honor the Son just as they honor the Father. Whoever does not honor the Son does not honor the Father, who sent him (John 5:19–23).

Reflection

Jesus is the way, the truth, and the life. If we hope to find fulfillment in existence, we need to follow him. He is the way that leads to joy; all other paths are false. Joy can only be found in doing God's will. When we are not in the flow of the divine will, we are heading to disaster, whether we know it or not, and being in that flow, we must know the Son. He is the way to the Father.

Replying to Moses from the burning bush on Sinai, when Moses asked his name, God replied: "I am who I am" (Exodus 3:14). Only God "is"; all other things, and all of us, participate in being only by sharing God's is-ness. Jesus is the truth that lies at the heart of all things; he was "in the beginning," we hear in the prologue to the gospel of John, "and through him, all things were made" (John 1:2–3). All created things can lead us to the Father. Even if someone doesn't know the Christ of the Bible, they can know God through the eternal logos who, with the Father, participated in the creation of everything that came to be and now exists.

Jesus is life. From all eternity he is life itself, and sharing our human nature, he vests our mortal life with immortality. Jesus shows us the possibility of our being, he shows us that our human form was made to be a vessel for divinity. Jesus is the archetype; the human through all humanity learns what it can mean to be human. We have been made not for death but for life as God's children. We are, more than anything else, sons and daughters of God. We are brothers and sisters of Jesus, through whom we have life eternal.

Prayer

Lord Jesus, you are the one who died so that we might live, and you are the one who rose so that we might live eternally. Show us the way to the fullness of life. We would follow you as your disciples! Teach us, loving brother, to know the Father through you. Reveal the Father's will for us to us. Fill us with the Spirit of wisdom and counsel, the Spirit of courage and devotion to the truth. You were faithful to the Father, give us that graceful courage you had so that we might also be faithful. You hand compassion for the least, the lost, and the broken, open our hearts to your beloved little ones. You willingly journeyed to Jerusalem where you suffered and died for us: sinless in the sinner's stead. We would follow after you. Each day let us pick up our cross and follow you in the way of generosity, grace, and self-gift. We pray all this in your holy name. Amen.

Activity

- Provided you have your doctor's permission, fast today. As you fast, ask the Lord to deepen your compassion for our brothers and sisters throughout the world suffering from hunger. .
- Pray for doctors, nurses, and others in the healing professions.

Prayer Journal and Notes

Thursday of the Fourth Week of Lent

Scripture Reading

"Very truly I tell you, whoever hears my word and believes him who sent me has eternal life and will not be judged but has crossed over from death to life. Very truly I tell you, a time is coming and has now come when the dead will hear the voice of the Son of God and those who hear will live. For as the Father has life in himself, so he has granted the Son also to have life in himself. And he has given him authority to judge because he is the Son of man" (John 5:24–27).

Reflection

Hear, believe, and live. It seems so simple. Hear the words of Jesus—but hearing is more than listening. When we hear something, we incorporate it into our lives. Hearing, in this sense, involves learning. The scribes and Pharisees may have listened to Jesus, but his disciples heard him.

Jesus's words reveal the glory of the Father who holds nothing back from his beloved, if flawed, creation. Jesus is the suffering servant who teaches that the Son of man must suffer, because it is in suffering that he reveals the depths of God's love for sinners. Jesus speaks words of life when he tells us that, if we want to be his disciples, his students, we must "pick up our cross daily" and follow him in a lifestyle of self-gift.

Jesus's words make little sense unless we believe in him and, through him, in the Father who sent him. Believe here does not mean an assent of the mind to propositional truth; it means to be in relationship with Jesus and the Father. Jesus is not talking about what we think, he is talking about who we are. We are to believe in Jesus' love for us; belief in our dignity as children of God; trust that the Spirit abides with us and lives within us as the center of our souls.

When we hear Jesus's words in this way and believe in him and the Father, we have eternal life now. Eternal life is something that will come to us in the great beyond when we hear and believe we are eternally alive in Christ.

Prayer

Father God, thank you for your providential love. You fill our days with your compassion and our nights with your peace. Give us ears to hear the words of Jesus, inviting us to follow him on the way of the cross. Help us to learn from him—from his humility and kindness, his love for even the least of our brothers and sisters. Jesus shows us our face, Father; when we see him, we see you. We believe that Jesus is your anointed one and that in his death and resurrection, he has set us free and made us your sons and daughters. We believe in your love, in your grace and forgiveness. We could not earn your love, and we could not, on our own, merit eternal life. What we could never get you have freely given us in overflowing abundance. We live, now, in your Son. He lives in us, and through him, we have life eternal, and we have it now. For this, we are eternally grateful. We pray through Jesus and in the Spirit, one God with you forever and ever. Amen.

Activity

- Spend an hour reading and reflecting on the fifth chapter of John's Gospel. How does Jesus explain his authority to heal? What does this teach us today? Write about this in your prayer journal.
- Pray for your pastor and for all ministers of the Gospel.

Prayer Journal and Notes

Friday of the Fourth Week of Lent

Scripture Reading

Many are the woes of the wicked,
but the Lord's unfailing love
surrounds the one who trusts in him.
Rejoice in the Lord and be glad, you righteous;
sing, all you who are upright in heart! (Psalm 32:10–11).

Reflection

Sin is its own punishment. In his letter to the Galatians, Paul writes, "Do not be deceived: God cannot be mocked. A man reaps what he sows" (Galatians 6:7). When we sow wickedness, we will reap a harvest of destruction. Paul goes on to write that "whoever sows to please the Spirit, from the Spirit will reap eternal life" (Galatians 6:8).

Simply put, our thoughts and actions have consequences, and the consequences attendant to sinful actions are dire. While sin may, for the moment, give us something that we desire, the long-term result will be emptiness. Elsewhere, Paul writes that "the wages of sin is death" (Romans 6:23).

Goodness is its own reward. When we do what the Lord expects of us, we are at peace. Even when we don't have all the "stuff" the world tells us we should long for, we have something more precious: a sense of being right with the world. This is the peace that surpasses all understanding, which our Jewish brothers and sisters call shalom. It is God's own peace, and it can come from him alone.

When we are in the right place (righteous), we can and should rejoice! The problem is that few of us are entirely upright, and few are thoroughly wicked. We are complex; sometimes we rise to the occasion and do the right thing, even when it's challenging to do so; but sometimes we are weak and slip easily into our habitual sins. Then what do we do?

The Gospel gives us hope. Jesus did not come to condemn but to save. God sent his Son to redeem sinful humanity and to forgive us over and over again if need be. The forgiveness of God is not earned or merited; it is gifted; it is pure grace. So even in our sinfulness, we can rejoice in the Lord for the salvation that is ours in Jesus Christ, and we can continue to struggle to live lives that are worthy of our high calling. Tarnished though we may be, we are image-bearers of God; we belong to him and to one another.

Prayer

Father, when we sin, we hurt ourselves and those who are closest to us. Sin brings trouble and pain and leads away from you and from your love into a dark place of lonely selfishness. We long to do your will, but our flesh is weak, and we sow seeds of our own destruction when we forget your law of love and act sinfully and selfishly. Forgive us, saving God, and lead us in the ways of your everlasting love. Help us to sow what is pleasing to your Holy Spirit so that we might reap an abundant harvest in eternity. Give us hearts that rejoice and sing grateful songs to you. Surround us with your unfailing love. We ask this in Jesus's name and through your Holy Spirit. You are One God forever and ever. Amen.

Activity

- Make today a day of fasting and abstinence (as long as you have the approval of your physician to do so).
- Read and meditate on Psalm 51. Write about your thoughts in your prayer journal.
- Pray for the conversion of sinners.

Prayer Journal and Notes

Saturday of the Fourth Week of Lent

Scripture Reading

I had been like a gentle lamb led to the slaughter;
I did not realize that they had
plotted against me, saying,
"Let us destroy the tree and its fruit;
let us cut him off from the land of the living,
that his name be remembered no more."
But you, Lord Almighty, who judge righteously
and test the heart and mind,
let me see your vengeance on them,
for to you I have committed my cause (Jeremiah 11:19–20).

Reflection

When things were going badly for the prophets, they would lament their situation. Prophetic laments take the form of a complaint to the Lord about the way things are, coupled with an affirmation of the Lord's faithfulness in times of distress and a request for his help. In Jeremiah 11, we hear the prophet's first lament: God has sent him with a message of judgment upon the faithlessness of Israel. The people had broken the covenant and were disobedient to the God of their salvation. "Cursed is the one who does not obey the terms of this covenant!" he prophesies (Jeremiah 11:3).

Israel can respond to Jeremiah's proclamation of condemnation in one of two ways: it can acknowledge its guilt and repent, or it can reject the message and "kill the messenger." Israel chooses to do the latter. Jeremiah laments that he didn't see his rejection or suffering coming; from his perspective he was an innocent doing the job Hashem gave him. Nevertheless, the people the Lord sent him to plotted his destruction.

When you destroy a tree and its fruit, you destroy it utterly; the tree is cut down, and its fruit cannot generate new life. This is how Jeremiah feels Israel is treating him. His existence and his progeny are in danger. Those who hate him would grind him to dust because of the word of the Lord he brings.

Jeremiah himself had two options: he can be faithless to the Lord and remain silent, or he can continue to faithfully proclaim the word that the Lord gave him to announce. He chooses faithfulness even at the risk of his own life. The prophet makes an act of faith and trust in the Lord, who judges rightly and tests the heart and the mind. Though his message is not received and the messenger is set upon and attacked, Jeremiah will still do the work he has been given. The prophet trusts that, in the end, God's righteousness will prevail and his justice will triumph.

Jesus is also the Lamb led to the slaughter. He came to his own to announce the Father's favor and to proclaim the good news, but he was a threat to the powers of this world. Though he was tempted, he remained faithful to his calling. Knowing that he is going to Calvary and his passion, Jesus resolutely turns his gaze on Jerusalem. The crucified one appears to have been defeated by the world that never accepted him, but his resurrection establishes God's ultimate victory over death forever.

When the world condemns us for our faith, we can fold like a cheap suit and give in to the ones who clamor for us to "fix it" with the world's values. Those values, though, will never lead to life. The challenge of Jeremiah, and the challenge of the cross is to remain faithful to God, to Christ, and to God's law when it is inconvenient when we are misunderstood, and even when we are maligned and persecuted for the faith. In those moments, commit your cause to the Lord Almighty, who reads the minds and hearts of men and judges rightly.

Prayer

Just judge, you know my mind better than I do. I am a mystery even to myself, but you know me, you have probed my mind and heart and understand me in my innermost being. The world does not know you, it did not know your Son, and it will not understand me as I strive to be his disciple. Like Jeremiah and Jesus, I too am a lamb among wolves. I place my life in your hands; to you I entrust my cause. Do not let the evil ones around me utterly destroy me, and do not let me succumb to evil and embrace it by going along with the values and practices of this world. Help me to see your will clearly and know right from wrong. Then, give me the courage to stand up for your word and your way in a twisted and perverse world. I ask all this in Jesus' name and through the Spirit he sent to abide with his people until the end of the ages. With you, they are Lord forever and ever. Amen.

Activity

- Examine your conscience. In what ways have you stood against the world and its values, and in what ways have you given in?
- Meditate on how you can better "stand for" the Gospel of Christ: what does the world embrace that denies the teachings of the Lord as we find them in scripture? Write about this in your prayer journal.
- Christians are being persecuted around the world, how can you help them with your prayer, and with your actions. *Do something,* even something small, to help someone suffering for the faith.
- Look at the Voice of the Martyrs website for ideas: https://www.persecution.com/.

Prayer Journal and Notes

Chapter 6

Fifth Week of Lent

Fifth Sunday of Lent

Scripture Reading

"Forget the former things;
do not dwell on the past.
See, I am doing a new thing!
Now it springs up; do you not perceive it?
I am making a way in the wilderness
and streams in the wasteland.
The wild animals honor me,
the jackals and the owls,
because I provide water in the wilderness
and streams in the wasteland,
to give drink to my people, my chosen,
the people I formed for myself
that they may proclaim my praise (Isaiah 43:18–21).

Reflection

Israel has been in exile and has suffered tremendously for its faithlessness to God and the covenant, but now the Lord is doing a new thing. The God who saved Israel from Pharaoh is now about to save his people again, this time from the Babylonians. Isaiah announces the Lord's saving acts. "Forget the former things," the prophet says. Don't look back. God acts in the present and asks us to look forward to his saving acts in the future. It would be a mistake to get lost in the past and think the Lord will always do what he always did. Don't dwell on what was, focus on what is. The Lord acts *now* in the life of his people.

The Lord who promises to "make all things new" is about to do a new thing—in fact, he is already doing it. "Do you not see it?" the prophet asks. The power of the Lord surrounds us, the earth is full of his majesty and power. He is acting now to rescue his people from all that holds them enslaved. Unless we look, though, we may be oblivious to God working in our midst.

The Lord does a new thing, and it would be a mistake to think that just because God has acted one way in the past, he will always work that way. God constantly does new things; he is the God of novelty and surprises. So don't miss him when he acts, and don't put him in a box. God will be who he will be, and our responsibility is to cooperate with his grace with grateful hearts. He brings the wilderness of our life back to life; he brings water to our arid places. He gives us all good things so that we may proclaim his praise forever.

Prayer

Creator God, you continue to create, each day you bless our world, and you bless our lives, with the new gifts of your love. No day is like any other; no two people are alike. Your handiwork is amazingly beautiful and unique. Thank you for making us who we are, and thank you for giving us the gift of each other: you give us spouses and partners, children and parents, neighbors and friends. Each one is your precious child, and each reveals your creative love. Open our eyes to your wonders all around us. Especially when we are in the wilderness of life, when we feel dry, lifeless, and along, help us to see your Spirit transforming the desert into a garden of new life and hope. You are a great God, and your love continues to astound and surprise us. For all this, let our lips and our lives give you praise and thanksgiving. All this, we pray in Jesus's name. Amen.

Activity

- In your prayer journal, make a list of what you are grateful for in your life. Spend an hour in prayer, giving thanks and praise to God for who and what you are. Write about this experience in your prayer journal.
- What new things is God doing in your life right now? Write about this in your prayer journal too.
- What things of the past do you need to let go of? How can you begin to free yourself from them? Take some concrete action steps in that direction: forgive an old offense and let go of it; write to someone who needs to hear from you. You know who it is!

Prayer Journal and Notes

_____

_____

_____

_____

_____

_____

_____

_____

_____

_____

_____

_____

_____

_____

_____

_____

_____

Monday of the Fifth Week of Lent

Scripture Reading

When Jesus spoke again to the people, he said, "I am the light of the world. Whoever follows me will never walk in darkness, but will have the light of life" (John 8:12).

Reflection

Without light, no one can see. Have you ever been in a completely dark room? If so, you know that it is impossible to see anything; without light, we are blind, we can see nothing. Jesus is the light of the world. Without Jesus, the world is in complete spiritual darkness. Only he can heal our blindness and enable us to see. Jesus brings light to the eyes of our hearts and allows us to glimpse things as they are in the sight of God. Without the light of Christ, we may have sight, but we lack insight.

The light Jesus brings is not only for seeing; it is also for "walking." When Christ lights up our minds and hearts, he gives us the light to travel safely through life by following him and thereby "walking in the light." When we have the light of Christ within us we, Jesus's disciples, are also light in the world. Jesus gives us our vocation when he explains his own. We are to be like Christ; we are to be light to the world, salt of the earth.

Prayer

Father, your Son Jesus brings light to the world. His light started shining at the very dawn of creation when the Word was with you participating in your creativity. His light shines in everything that was made: things animate and inanimate. All things shine forth with divine light, all things reveal your wisdom and love. The full radiance of your light shines forth in your Son Jesus. On the cross, his light reaches to the ends of the earth as he reveals the depth, and height, and width, and breadth of your love. Make our light also, reflecting the light of the Son. He is Lord with you in the Spirit forever and ever. Amen.

Activity

- How can you *be* the light of Christ? Meditate on ways you can bring the light to others with whom you come in contact.
- Being the light requires us to reflect the Son. How can we better be images of God in Christ? Write about this in your prayer journal.
- Do something to help the disadvantaged in your community. Don't just give money (though that's okay too); spend your time helping neighbors in need. As you do, remember that in them, you see Christ.

Prayer Journal and Notes

Tuesday of the Fifth Week of Lent

Scripture Reading
"I have much to say in judgment of you. But he who sent me is trustworthy, and what I have heard from him I tell the world."

They did not understand that he was telling them about his Father. So Jesus said, "When you have lifted up the Son of man, then you will know that I am he and that I do nothing on my own but speak just what the Father has taught me. The one who sent me is with me; he has not left me alone, for I always do what pleases him" (John 8:26–29).

Reflection
All that we know of the Father we learn from Jesus. He is the perfect likeness of the invisible, immortal, all-wise God. When we hear Jesus teach, we are listening to the Father; when we see Jesus heal, we are seeing the power of the Father; when we see Jesus's compassion for the brokenhearted and for sinners, we are seeing the heart of the Father.

On the cross, where the Son of man is lifted up, we know the fullness of the Father's love. The cross is where the glory of God is most clearly revealed. This is *not* glory as the world understands it; worldly glory comes with parades, and marching bands, and pomp. Earthly glory looks majestic. The cross is not majestic. While we have sanitized it over the millennia, the cross was originally a tool of humiliating torture and death. If the Roman Empire wanted to make an example of some troublemaker, they crucified him.

Crucifixion was humiliating, public, painful, and slow. The condemned criminal hung naked and brutalized for hours until death ended his torment. People would come out and watch, and mock, and the best among them would tremble within as they watched a fellow human being's life taken with cynical cruelty. And this, *this*, is the glory of God.

The crucifixion is God's glory because, in it, Jesus shows his obedience to the Father's love for God's broken creation. Jesus puts off his divinity, takes on our humanity, forgoes comfort and dignity, suffers painfully, and then pours out the last drop of his blood because he loves us. In this outpouring of self-gift (grace), Christ freely chose to take on the burden of our sin and pay its price as a ransom for us. God is love, and the glory of God shines forth in the great act of divine love: the cross of our Savior.

We must never cease being grateful.

Prayer

Lord Jesus, your cross sets us free. You suffered and died because of your great love for us, all of us and each of us. Thank you for your saving love. Keep our sin before us so that we can remember your love and revel in your forgiveness. You show us who the Father is; you show us that God *is* love, that God cares for us, and that even when we feel far away from you and your kingdom, you are near; you are with us, you will always be with us, and you will never leave us. Fill us with the Spirit of understanding so that we may live in awe of your lovingkindness. Through the Spirit, transform us into other Christs so that we might also reveal the love of the Father to a suffering, sinful world. We ask this in your name and through the Spirit. With the Father, you are one God forever and ever. Amen.

Activity

- Meditate on the cross. Write your insights in your prayer journal.
- As Jesus's disciples, we must "pick up our cross daily." What does that mean for you, practically, in your daily life? How does your cross call you to change? Do something today that expresses your commitment to the cross. Be creative. Record this in your prayer journal.

Prayer Journal and Notes

Wednesday of the Fifth Week of Lent

Scripture Reading
Jesus said, "If you hold to my teaching, you are really my disciples. Then you will know the truth, and the truth will set you free" (John 8:31–32).

Reflection
The promise the Lord makes here is conditional: to receive the promised benefits we must first abide in his word. The word "abide" has the sense of "remaining." When we abide somewhere, we make it our dwelling place. Jesus is inviting us to become steeped in our relationship with him: he is the Logos, who was present at the beginning. He has sent us his Spirit to abide with us and in us until the end of the ages; to truly be his disciple, we must abide in his Spirit.

The discipleship Jesus is speaking of here is experiential. We are not to learn information and ideas; we are to become like the teacher through his presence in our lives. In Jesus's time, students would live with their teacher, learning to be like him—to think as he thought, to act as he acted, and to pray as he prayed. Jesus invites us into a similar relationship with him in the Spirit.

When that Spirit becomes our center—the heart of our heart— then Jesus promises three things: first, we will indeed be his disciples. Being present to Jesus in the Spirit is the *only* way to learn from the master. The deeper we go in this relationship, the more we learn, and the more we grow in Christ.

Second, when we abide in the word, we will know the truth not, as some might think, as an abstract principle, but as a person. Jesus is the truth. We know what is true only by reference to him, the fixed point in an otherwise changing universe. He is the lodestar; solely by reference to him can we safely journey to life into the freedom of the sons and daughters of God.

Third, our presence to the abiding Spirit is the only path that leads to freedom. Jesus is the truth that sets us free. In Christ alone can our souls be free to be and do that for which we were created. This is the essence of genuine freedom.

Prayer

Abiding Spirit, be the heart of our heart, the soul of our soul, the mind of our mind. Draw us into an abiding relationship with the word made flesh, and through that relationship transform us: shape our thoughts so that they are the thoughts of our teacher; shape our hearts so that we can love as Jesus loved; soften our words so that we might speak his truth and know his ways. Give us the grace to follow him in every respect. Remind us to spend time in prayer and in communion with the one who, alone is liberating truth: Jesus, our brother and our savior. We ask all this through you, Spirit God, and through the one who sent you to us. Together with the Father, you are one God forever and ever. Amen.

Activity

- Spend an hour in solitude/silence and reflect on the word present within you.
- Take a walk in a quiet place and be aware of the presence of God in nature.
- Reflect on ways in which you can deepen your likeness to Christ. Write about this in your prayer journal.

Prayer Journal and Notes

Thursday of the Fifth Week of Lent

Scripture Reading

The Lord is my Shepherd, I lack nothing.
He makes me lie down in green pastures,
he leads me beside quiet waters,
He refreshes my soul.
He guides me along the right paths
for his name's sake.
Even though I walk
through the darkest valley,
I will fear no evil,
for you are with me;
your rod and your staff,
they comfort me.
You prepare a table before me
in the presence of my enemies.
You anoint my head with oil;
my cup overflows.
Surely your goodness and love will follow me
all the days of my life,
and I will dwell in the house of the Lord
forever (Psalm 23).

Reflection

Psalm 23 is one of the most recognizable poems in world literature; even people with no religious training recognize the hope-filled words of David: "The Lord is my shepherd, I lack nothing." Millions of people throughout the millennia have been comforted at times of loss by the psalmist's fearless confidence in the face of death's dark valley. Beyond the darkness, the psalm affirms God's faithful loving kindness throughout life and into eternity, where he is promised a dwelling place in Shepherd's home "forever."

What is the source of this profound optimism? The language of the 23rd psalm gives us some hints. Shepherd and shepherding were frequent metaphors, in the ancient world, for the kings and rulers of peoples; Ezekiel condemns the shepherds of Israel as those who took care only of themselves and failed in their mission to strengthen the weak, heal the sick, and bring back the strays. Condemning them for their failures, God says: "I myself will tend my sheep" (Ezekiel 34:15). The Lord is the one who will "rescue the sheep from the places they have been scattered" (Ezekiel 34:12).

What can we learn about this divine Shepherd? The word for "shepherd" in Hebrew is *ra'ah*. It is etymologically connected to *re'eh*, which means "friend." When David takes heart because the Lord is his Shepherd, he is also acknowledging the deeper relationship of friend that he has with the one who walks with him through the dark valley. He fears no evil because the one with him is not only his Shepherd, tending him, leading him, protecting him, and restoring him; that Shepherd is his friend, one who cares for him deeply with bonds of loyalty and love.

Jesus, the Good Shepherd, walks with us through every moment of our lives: he is with us in times of darkness and times of joy; times of suffering and times of ecstasy. He doesn't call us servants; he calls us his friends (John 15:15). He reveals himself fully to us and knows us fully. Even when we are unaware, he is there: guiding, strengthening, and loving us; supplying our every need, giving us courage in times of darkness, and inviting us to dwell with him in our true home forever.

Prayer

Shepherd of Israel, guide us in safe paths. We know you are always with us even when we don't feel your presence. You care for us tenderly and restore our spirits when they flag. Heal our brokenness, fill us with gratitude for your love, and allow us to help you bring others into your fold so that there will be one flock and one shepherd. We pray this in your holy name. Amen.

Activity

- Slowly pray and meditate on Psalm 23. What does it reveal to you about God? About yourself? Write about this in your prayer journal.
- What are some ways in which you can help the Good Shepherd in his mission to restore the lost, heal the broken, and give strength to the weak? As Jesus's disciples, we are called to assist him in his shepherding ministry—we are like his sheepdogs!

Prayer Journal and Notes

Friday of the Fifth Week of Lent

Scripture Reading

"The works I do in my Father's name testify about me, but you do not believe because you are not my sheep. My sheep listen to my voice; I know them, and they follow me. I give them eternal life, and they shall never perish; no one will snatch them out of my hand. My Father, who has given them to me, is greater than all; no one can snatch them out of my Father's hand. The Father and I are one" (John 10:25–30).

Reflection

Jesus shows us everything we can know about the Father: he and the Father are one and the same. When we see Jesus, we see God in God's fullness; when we hear Jesus, we listen to the voice of God; when are touched by the presence of Jesus's Spirit in our lives, we are moved by God.

If Jesus is the Good Shepherd, then we, his disciples, are the sheep of his fold. Sheep, the real ones, are helpless animals. They have no natural defenses; they don't bite, they have no horns, and they are vulnerable creatures in peril whenever they are apart from their shepherd.

We too are in danger when we are separated from the Shepherd. Our life depends on hearing his voice and following where he leads.

We listen to his voice in scripture. To be his sheep and to listen to his voice, we must be in the scriptures daily, not merely reading but meditating on the words we hear in the sacred texts, and especially in the Gospels that tell us the story of Jesus's life, death, and resurrection. A meditative reading of scripture requires that we slowly go through the words of the sacred authors—pausing on words to allow them to evoke meaning from deep within us.

The Shepherd's words reveal the Shepherd. As we pray, we learn to know our Shepherd/friend. The better we know Jesus, the more deeply we will trust and follow him, even into strange and unknown places. It is only by following the Shepherd, though, that we can find safe pasture—a meaningful and joyous existence in this world, and in the next—eternal life.

Prayer

Good Shepherd, open our ears to your voice. Help us to listen to you and obey your call as you beckon us to come and follow you. We know that you do not promise us lives of ease and comfort; there may be dangers and suffering on the roads you call us to walk. When we take up our cross we know we will die with you, but only so that we can also rise with you. Give us the courage to follow you and trust in your Spirit within us. Let your Spirit be the compass within us that points us to you and to eternal life. You promise that, once we are yours, we will never perish and nothing well be able to snatch us out of your hands. Take us into your saving, nail-pierced hands, and never let us be parted from you: not be sin, not by danger, not by persecution, not by death. We are yours, and you are the Father's, and he is all. Amen.

Activity

- Spend some time prayerfully meditating on John 10:25–30. What is that passage challenging you to do? How is it challenging for you to change?
- What practices of discipleship might you want to incorporate into your daily routine so that you will be better able to hear the voice of the Shepherd? Write about this in your prayer journal.

Prayer Journal and Notes

_____

_____

_____

_____

_____

_____

_____

_____

_____

_____

_____

_____

_____

_____

_____

_____

Saturday of the Fifth Week of Lent

Scripture Reading

"Lord," Martha said to Jesus, "if you had been here, my brother would not have died. But I know that even now God will give you whatever you ask.

Jesus said to her, "Your brother will rise again."

Martha answered, "I know he will rise again in the resurrection at the last day."

Jesus said to her, "I am the resurrection and the life. The one who believes in me will live, even though they die; and whoever lives by believing in me will never die. Do you believe this?" (John 11:21–26).

Reflection

We live in a culture of death; it is all around us. Open any newspaper, and you'll find disaster stories galore. "If it bleeds, it leads," journalists say of their penchant for reporting on the bloody tales of disaster and death that we find so troubling and so fascinating. We hide from death by packing our elderly off to nursing homes where we need not see them as they grow older and feebler. Who wants to be reminded where they are so we will be if we have the good fortune to live to old age?

On the other end of the spectrum, we cavalierly dispose of unwanted and inconvenient life, euphemizing the process by calling it "choice," and pretending it is a good thing, a right, a woman's right to kill off the child of her womb. What have we become?

We want to live, but our culture has forgotten what real life is. We think it's a license to do what we want, forgetting that true freedom is not doing as we please, but doing what is right, what is good, what is pleasing to the Author of life. Unless we are obedient to his will, we choose death and emptiness. We are surrounded by the walking dead who follow the clarion call of our culture: do what is convenient, what is self-satisfying, what gives you momentary pleasure. Forget, as you do so, that you are, in Heidegger's phrase,

"Being unto death," that we are daily growing closer to the moment when we will no longer "be."

"Waste your precious time," this age calls to us. "You have plenty of time—all the time in the world."

But we don't.

Yet there is one who says, "The one who believes in me will live, even though they die; and those who live believing in me will never die" (John 11:25–26). We should ask ourselves the question Jesus poses to Martha of Bethany: Do you believe this? Jesus is the key to life—to our life and to the world's life. If, and only if, we believe in him, we will never die. For the Christian, the death of our bodies is just another day, one where we pass from life to life. In the risen Lord, the one who died and now lives, we have our hope of escaping the culture of death and becoming part of the kingdom of life that is always "in your midst" (Luke 17:21).

The key to life is a vibrant, faith-filled relationship with Jesus, who is "the way, the truth, and the life" (John 14:6). Life-giving faith is not a head trip. Life-giving faith is active; it takes risks; it says no to death and to the culture of death. Life-giving faith brings good news to the poor and values life wherever it is found, from the moment of conception to the hour of natural death. Life-giving faith is selfless faith; it lets go of selfishness and doesn't cling to "stuff." Rather, it values what the Father values and lives each moment living fully in obedience to him. Jesus shows us the way: he is the way. He reveals the truth; he is the truth, and he promises us that we will never die, for he is the life.

Prayer

Creator God, you are Lord of the living, the author of all life. We give you thanks for quickening our spirit within us today and every day. Your love for us knows no boundaries. Give us awe for your creative genius and give us eyes to see the wonders with which you surround us. Faithful God, give us reverence for life in all its forms. Let our own life reflect your glory and your love. Help us to live every moment of our existence in obedience to you and to your Spirit. We pray this in Jesus's name. Amen.

Activity

- Take a walk in a quiet place and meditate on the wonders of creation. Let your mind focus on the beauty and diversity of life around you.
- Later in the evening, reflect on your prayer walk in your prayer journal.
- What are some of the ways that you can live your own life more fully? Write them down.
- What changes might this require in your daily routine?

Prayer Journal and Notes

_____

_____

_____

_____

_____

_____

_____

_____

_____

_____

_____

_____

_____

_____

_____

_____

_____

Chapter 7

Holy Week

Palm Sunday

Scripture Reading

As he approached Jerusalem and saw the city, he wept over it and said, "If you, even you, had only known on this day what would bring you peace—but now it is hidden from your eyes. The days will come upon you when your enemies will build an embankment against you and encircle you and hem you in on every side. They will dash you to the ground, you and the children within your walls. They will not leave one stone on another, because you did not recognize the time of God's coming to you" (Luke 19:41–44).

Reflection

Jerusalem failed to recognize the day of God's visitation. Jesus, the incarnate Son, came to his people, to Jerusalem, but went unrecognized. God wasn't enough like what the people expected God to be like. God is awesome, glorious, and mighty; no one can look upon God's face and live. Is it any wonder that when a poor, itinerant preacher shows up, from Galilee, no less, no one would recognize him as the presence of the divinity in human flesh.

We humans tend to think in familiar patterns, and if something doesn't fit the model, it will confuse us, at best. We might even reject it. We tend not to see what we don't look for or expect to see, nor do we look for things where we don't expect them to be. Jerusalem completely missed the time of God's coming, and so, often, do we. We miss Jesus when he comes to us through the poor, the suffering, the lonely, and the broken. We fail to see Jesus calling to us in the dark places of our world where our human eyes only see suffering and confusion.

Jesus weeps over a Jerusalem that failed to see who he really was, and as he did, he wept too for all his brothers and sisters throughout the ages who would be unable to have the vision to recognize the Spirit of God coming to us in unexpected ways, at unlikely times, though unforeseen people. When we reject the inconvenient prophets who call us to see God's presence differently, we reject the Lord who sent them. When we don't help the sick, the oppressed, the imprisoned, or the marginalized, we fail to help the Lord himself.

We must be vigilant, watchful, and attentive, because the Lord will come at a time and in a way that we least expect. Make no mistake about it, though, he will come to us. He already has.

Prayer

Lord, you come to us in the quiet times when we take time to listen for your still, small voice; you come to us in the hustle and bustle of our workaday lives. You come to us through our spouses, our children, our friends, and our neighbors. When we encounter the sorrowing or suffering of others, we meet your suffering face in them. Lord, make us sensitive to your presence and aware of you in every encounter, with every person, in every situation of our lives. Let your Spirit of discernment fill us so that we may never fail to see and welcome you when you come to us. Come, Lord Jesus, today and every day until, on that last day, you come to us in your glory. Amen.

Activity

- Reflect on the last twenty-four hours. When have you seen the presence of God? How did he appear to you? When did you first realize the Lord was with you? How did you greet or welcome him?

- When have you missed seeing Christ in the events or encounters of your life? When did you realize you missed him? What can you do to see him more clearly when he next comes to you? Write about all this in your prayer journal.

Prayer Journal and Notes

Monday of Holy Week

Scripture Reading

"Here is my servant, whom I uphold,
my chosen one in whom I delight;
I will put my Spirit on him,
and he will bring justice to the nations.
He will not shout or cry out,
or raise his voice in the streets.
A bruised reed he will not break,
and a smoldering wick he will not snuff out.
In faithfulness he will bring forth justice;
he will not falter or be discouraged
till he establishes justice on earth.
In his teaching the islands will put their hope" (Isaiah 42:1–4).

Reflection

God does things differently than we do. Here we have the Lord of the universe, the One whose name is so sacred that it is unutterable; no one can look upon his face and live. His plan is nothing less than to bring justice to the earth, his creation that has so strayed that injustice abounds. Instead of truth, the Lord looks everywhere and sees selfishness, greed, and unkindness. The meek are trampled, the weak are exploited, and the helpless find no help at all. The problem of injustice is huge and chronic.

In the face of the tremendous problem of sin and injustice throughout creation, God sends his servant, his chosen one; God anoints that chosen servant with the Spirit. We can expect things to happen, and they do, just not always the things for which we hope. Instead of power, the Servant is gentle; he doesn't cry out or shout; he is gentle with the broken and hurting. He is patient with the weak and persistent in his message of hope, which will be brought to the ends of the earth.

It is not Jesus's power and might that brings justice to the earth, it is his faithfulness to the One who sent him. Israel expected a conquering hero, and we expect vindication from the heavens: but we get love, we get the faithfulness of the suffering servant, we get the crucified God. In pouring out his life in obedience to the Father, Jesus has established God's kingdom on earth. Justice has come, and the Chosen One now reigns: not as an earthly King with triumphant power, but like the heavenly King, who patiently gathers the strays, seeks out the lost, and binds up the wounds of the sinful and suffering.

Prayer

Father, thank you for sending us your Son Jesus to be our brother and our savior. His gentle compassion shows us your face: you are the one who loves tenderly and patiently. Your passion for justice is revealed in your love for the small things of our world: for children, for those who wander through life not really understanding how or where they fit in. You love those whom others reject and deny, and you rejoice when your children are patient and understanding of each other. Put your Spirit on us so that we, like Jesus, might bring justice to the earth through our faithfulness to you. We ask this in Jesus's name, with you and the Spirit he is one God forever and ever. Amen.

Activity

Pray for the victims of injustice in our world. What are some ways you can improve their lot? Do something to bring justice to the earth. Write about the experience in your prayer journal.

Take some concrete action to enhance justice in your own community (e.g., volunteer at a soup kitchen, food pantry, or a place that provides meals for the homeless; visit an elderly friend at a nursing home, or "adopt a grandparent" who you can visit).

Prayer Journal and Notes

_____

_____

_____

_____

_____

_____

_____

_____

_____

_____

_____

_____

_____

_____

_____

_____

_____

Tuesday of Holy Week

Scripture Reading

Jesus knew that the Father had put all things under his power and that he had come from God and was returning to God; so he got up from the meal, took off his outer clothing, and wrapped a towel around his waist. After that, he poured water into a basin and began to wash his disciples' feet, drying them with the towel that was wrapped around him.

He came to Simon Peter, who said to him, "Lord, are you going to wash my feet?"

Jesus replied, "You do not realize now what I am doing, but later, you will understand."

"No," said Peter, "you shall never wash my feet."

Jesus answered, "Unless I wash you, you have no part with me."

"Then, Lord," Simon Peter replied, "not just my feet but my hands and my head as well!" (John 13:3–9).

Reflection

Jesus redefines leadership as service. On the night before he died, he gave his disciples, including us, an example to follow. He was the teacher and Lord, and now he is on the verge of completing his mission from the Father. His followers now see him as the Messiah, the long-awaited savior, and liberator. He is the presence of God in human form, and they are beginning to realize this. God's ways, however, are not ours. The one who is master and Lord has come to be the servant of all, and to empty himself in obedience to God and in service to his brothers and sisters.

When Jesus wraps a towel around himself and moves from disciple to disciple, washing their feet, he is doing the work of a slave: dirty work. This symbolic foot washing was a sign of the cleansing that occurs as Jesus washes us in the blood of the cross, cleansing us for all time and establishing a bond between himself and his followers who become "united to him in likeness to his death." We are invited too to become servants, to figuratively wash each other's feet, and to pour out our own selves in service to our brothers and sisters.

As Christians, we are called to serve, and our leaders are called to be the servant of the servants. Jesus shows us the way when he washes the feet of his disciples, and as he takes up his cross and gives his life for the sins of the world. When we serve one another, when we take up our cross, die to ourselves, and follow him, we become one with him in his lifestyle of self-gift.

Prayer

Lord, your love and generosity are our salvation. As you washed the feet of your disciples the night before you died, so you wash us with the blood of the cross. You have given everything in obedience to the Father and out of love for your beloved friends. Thank you that you call us friends. Thank you for revealing the Father's love. Thank you for showing us that God is love, selfless, self-giving love. Fill us with your Spirit so that we, your disciples, might live like you, love like you, and serve like you. We pray all this in your name. Amen.

Activity

- In meditation, imagine what it feels like to have Jesus wash your feet. Picture yourself at table with him when he wrapped the towel around himself, poured water in a basin, and went from disciple to disciple. See him kneel down in front of you, feel him pour the water over your feet as he bathes them, and then feel him take the towel and dry your feet. What are you thinking as this happens? What does this teach you? How does this change you?
- How can you emulate Jesus's service? Who in your community needs the tender care and love that only you can give?
- Write about this in your prayer journal.

Prayer Journal and Notes

_____

_____

_____

_____

_____

_____

_____

_____

_____

_____

_____

_____

_____

_____

_____

_____

_____

Wednesday of Holy Week

Scripture Reading

Then one of the twelve—the one called Judas Iscariot—went to the chief priests and asked, "What are you willing to give me if I deliver him over to you?" So they counted out for him thirty pieces of silver. From then on, Judas watched for an opportunity to hand him over (Matthew 26:14–16).

Reflection

We don't know much about Judas Iscariot, though his name has become synonymous with betrayal. He was a disciple of Jesus, one of the twelve, who was called by the Lord to follow him. Accepting the invitation, Judas traveled with Jesus, saw the Lord work wonders of healing and deliverance, and heard him teach with authority about the love of God. While he was not one of Jesus's inner circle, he was Jesus's friend. What caused him to turn? How did Satan use him, and why did it work?

Judas was the money guy; he kept the common purse for Jesus and the others, and John tells us Judas wasn't trustworthy. He helped himself to the money. Like most embezzlers, this probably started small, taking a little bit here and there to cover some personal expenses. Then it grew, and the more he got away with, the more he felt emboldened to steal. Money became more important to Judas than Jesus, than God. Money was his idol.

When the opportunity to cash in on his position as one of the twelve presented itself, Judas took it. He might not have thought that the end of his betrayal would be the crucifixion of his friend. He might even have thought that turning Jesus over to the authorities would force Jesus to play his hand and fulfill his messianic role. Jesus would reveal his power, become King, and get rid of the Romans once and for all. Like the others, Judas didn't understand that Jesus was not going to be the Messiah they wanted but the Messiah God wanted.

Thirty pieces of silver would be worth between $12,000 and

$15,000 today. While that's not a lot of money, it's enough to tempt a greedy man with compromised integrity to betray a friend. Satan used Judas's greed and dishonesty to seduce and ultimately destroy him.

It is easy to point the finger at Judas, but it would be more profitable to try to learn from him and his mistakes. What are the weaknesses Satan uses to compromise us? How have we betrayed Jesus in the way we treat each other? What idols do we serve—money (like Judas did), pleasure, power, lust?

Prayer

Lord, you call us to follow you faithfully, but we often turn away from you toward idols of our choosing. We are fooled by the empty pleasures and promises of the world and pursue them while ignoring our relationship with you. Like Judas, we sell our souls for fading pleasures and squander your gifts of life and love. Forgive us, saving Lord, and guide us back to the path of righteousness. Make our spirits hunger and thirst for you and your kingdom. Amen.

Activity

- Examine your conscience: what "gods" are you serving instead of the Living God? How can you reorganize your life's priorities to become more faithful to Jesus and his Gospel?
- How can you make amends for your betrayals of Jesus? Be concrete and take action to change.
- Write about this in your prayer journal.

Prayer Journal and Notes

Maundy Thursday

Scripture Reading

When the hour came, Jesus and his apostles reclined at the table. And he said to them, "I have eagerly desired to eat this Passover with you before I suffer. For I tell you, I will not eat it again until it finds fulfillment in the kingdom of God."

After taking the cup, he gave thanks and said, "Take this and divide it among you. For I tell you I will not drink again from the fruit of the vine until the kingdom of God comes."

And he took bread, gave thanks and broke it, and gave it to them, saying, "This is my body given for you; do this in remembrance of me."

In the same way, after the supper he took the cup, saying, "This cup is the new covenant in my blood, which is poured out for you (Luke 22:14–20).

Reflection

Jesus's hour had come—the hour he was born for, the hour for completing his mission and revealing the fullness of God's love for his broken creation. Jesus was known for eating and drinking with sinners, for meal fellowship. In the culture of the time, long before McDonald's sold their first Big Mac, eating with others was a symbol of intimacy and acceptance. People ate with their families, their friends, but they would never eat with strangers, or with "sinners," and never, unless they couldn't help it, would they eat alone.

When Jesus invites tax collectors, prostitutes, and sinners to his table, he is saying these people too are children of God, beloved by the Father. While "polite society" may reject them as "deplorable," Jesus embraces them as brothers and sisters.

I'm reminded of Edwin Markham's poem "Outwitted":

"He drew a circle that shut me out—
Heretic, rebel, a thing to flout.

But love and I had the wit to win:
We drew a circle and took him in!"[7]

Jesus outwitted his enemies by loving them. The scribes and Pharisees, the Herodians and Sadducees, the elites who were hostile or cold to Jesus's message, even those who plotted to kill him—he loved them all. He loved them to death.

Prayer

We give you thanks, Lord, for your body broken for us and your blood shed for us. We thank you for the meal you gave us to remember your saving work and to make you present in our midst. We thank you because we, like the travelers on the road to Emmaus, can recognize you in the breaking of bread, and realize, as we do so, that you have been walking every step of our journey, even though we may not have realized it. Fill our hearts with gratitude, Saving Christ, and give us loving hearts, like yours, so that by sharing in your lifestyle of love and generosity, we might bring others to your table. We ask this in your name and through the Spirit. Amen.

Activity

- Prayerfully read Jesus's farewell discourse (all of John 14). What challenges do you find in it for your life today? Write about this in your prayer journal.
- Attend a service of the Lord's supper today at your church.
- Pray for unity among Christians.

---

[7] "Outwitted" by Edwin Markhan (blog post), retrieved January 29, 2008, from https://karenspoetryspot.blogspot.com/2008/01/outwitted-by-edwin-markham.html.

Prayer Journal and Notes

Good Friday

Scripture Reading

When they came to the place called the Skull, they crucified him there, along with the criminals—one on his right, the other on his left. Jesus said, "Father, forgive them, for they do not know what they are doing." And they divided up his clothes by casting lots.

The people stood watching, and the rulers even sneered at him. They said, "He saved others; let him save himself if he is God's Messiah, the Chosen One."

The soldiers also came up and mocked him. They offered him wine vinegar and said, "If you are the king of the Jews, save yourself."

There was a written notice above him, which read: this is the King of the Jews (Luke 23:33–38).

Reflection

Hannah Arendt, a Jewish philosopher during the twentieth century, wrote, "The discoverer of the role of forgiveness in the realm of human affairs was Jesus of Nazareth.[8]

Jesus's prayer from the cross, "Father, forgive them, for they do not know what they are doing" (Luke 23:34), is among the most important words ever uttered in human history. It sets the standard for love and forgiveness, and does so in deed as well as word. Jesus, in agony on the cross, looks down upon his tormenters and asks the Father to forgive them. In this he doesn't merely teach us the way, he shows us.

Listen to what he doesn't say. He doesn't say, "Father, forgive them if they sincerely apologize (and it better be sincere)"; nor does he say, "Father, forgive them once we settle the score." Jesus demonstrated love and forgiveness with no strings attached, and he does it in the most difficult of circumstances.

---

[8] Hannah Arendt, *The Human Condition* (Chicago: University of Chicago Press, 1958), 238.

Forgiveness is one of those things that is easy to talk about but difficult to do. We tend to cling to our sense of outrage when we feel ourselves to have been treated unjustly; we want to the right the scales of justice and think we can do that by holding onto our bitterness. That strategy doesn't work, it only succeeds in poisoning our spirit with anger and making us nastier and more cynical.

Jesus's prayer from the cross challenges us to forgive fully and from the heart, as he did. His prayer invites us to pray for those who have hurt us, even if they are unrepentant; even if they are persistent in their hostility toward us. If there is ever to be peace in our lives and souls, it will only come if we follow the Prince of Peace: as he forgave his murderers so must we forgive all who sin against us.

Only then will the world know that we are truly his disciples.

Prayer

Father, give us hearts which forgive as you have forgiven us, and we ask you, too, to forgive all who have sinned against us in any way. Help us to let go of any bitterness or anger which we might still feel toward anyone. Lord, clothe us with compassion, humility, and gentleness. Give us the grace we need to bear with others patiently and with kindness. Through your Spirit, enable us to live with a genuine love for others, a love like your Son's, with no strings attached. And may your own peace rule our hearts, since as your children we have been called to that peace. Finally, make us thankful for the gift of life that is ours in Christ Jesus. We make this prayer in his name through the power of the Spirit, they are one God with you forever and ever. Amen.

Activity

- Find a church that is open from noon to three and spend that time in prayer. During these three hours, read the passion accounts in all four Gospels.

- Do a spiritual inventory, and forgive anyone against whom you hold any grudge or hatred. Ask the Lord's help in letting go.
- Abstain from meat today.

Prayer Journal and Notes

_____

_____

_____

_____

_____

_____

_____

_____

_____

_____

_____

_____

_____

_____

_____

_____

_____

_____

Holy Saturday

Scripture Reading

Later, Joseph of Arimathea asked Pilate for the body of Jesus. Now Joseph was a disciple of Jesus, but secretly because he feared the Jewish leaders. With Pilate's permission, he came and took the body away. He was accompanied by Nicodemus, the man who earlier had visited Jesus at night. Nicodemus brought a mixture of myrrh and aloes, about seventy-five pounds. Taking Jesus's body, the two of them wrapped it, with the spices, in strips of linen. This was in accordance with Jewish burial customs. At the place where Jesus was crucified, there was a garden, and in the garden a new tomb, in which no one had ever been laid. Because it was the Jewish day of preparation and since the tomb was nearby, they laid Jesus there (John 19:38–42).

Reflection

He was really dead!

The expectations of his disciples died with him on that cross, dashed beyond any human repair. They thought he was the Messiah of God, but no Messiah would die like that: humiliated and tortured, on display for all as he died the shameful death of a criminal. No, he was just another murdered prophet.

The hopes of the marginalized also died that Friday afternoon on the hill outside Jerusalem: Jesus told them God loved them; that they were beloved in the sight of the God he called Father. What Father would let his son die feeling "forsaken," though? His message of love and inclusion for sinners and outcasts died with him on that cross, they were sure of that: who could take the message of a crucified Christ seriously?

His friends' hearts were broken, as were the hearts of those he helped and healed. Eyes to which he gave sight now streamed with tears! Their hearts burned when he taught them, now his voice was forever silent. He helped so many, but when it mattered, there was no one there to help him. His lifeless body taken down from the cross and laid in a borrowed tomb.

Now they were afraid. They might be the next victims of Rome or the establishment anxious to rid itself entirely of the problematic prophet and his followers. It was dangerous for them now, many hid out of fear, planning their escape from Jerusalem. Nothing could defeat their fear or quench their grief at losing him, but lose him they did, and with him was lost any lingering belief that Jesus was the Christ, the one who was to come.

It was over—or so they all thought.

Prayer

Lord, on this day when your friends and loved ones mourned for you, we too keep vigil as we wait to celebrate your resurrection. There is a somber stillness to this day when we remember the time your body was placed in the tomb and your friends, hearts broken and spirits crushed, hid in fear and confusion. Help us when our hearts are broken, when our spirits are crushed, and when we are confused because of the events of our lives. Unlike your friends on that first Holy Saturday, we know that you are risen, we know that you live, and we know that, because you live we also will live. Keep us close to you in moments of sadness, and lift our spirits. In the quiet of this day, make us one with all who suffer and grieve, and make us one, too, with your holy spirit. We pray all this in your holy name. Amen.

Activity

- Spend the afternoon quietly; read a book on spirituality, prayer, or the Bible. Read carefully and take notes in the margins. Write any insights you have in your prayer journal.
- Pray for people you know who are sad or grieving. Write one of them a note expressing your concern and support.
- If any of your loved ones are deceased, make a visit to their gravesite and place flowers there.

Prayer Journal and Notes

Chapter 8

Resurrection Sunday

The Resurrection of the Lord

Scripture Reading

Now Mary stood outside the tomb crying. As she wept, she bent over to look into the tomb and saw two angels in white, seated where Jesus's body had been, one at the head and the other at the foot.

They asked her, "Woman, why are you crying?"

"They have taken my Lord away," she said, "and I don't know where they have put him." At this, she turned around and saw Jesus standing there, but she did not realize that it was Jesus.

He asked her, "Woman, why are you crying? Who is it you are looking for?"

Thinking he was the gardener, she said, "Sir, if you have carried him away, tell me where you have put him, and I will get him."

Jesus said to her, "Mary."

She turned toward him and cried out in Aramaic, "Rabboni!" (which means "teacher").

Jesus said, "Do not hold on to me, for I have not yet ascended to the Father. Go instead to my brothers and tell them, 'I am ascending to my Father and your Father, to my God and your God.'"

Mary Magdalene went to the disciples with the news: "I have seen the Lord!" (John 20:11–18).

Reflection

Karl Matter retired from the Marine Corps at the rank of colonel after a lifetime of service to his country. Karl saw action in Desert Shield and Desert Storm; he served on General Mattis's senior staff and was deployed around the world throughout a long career.

Of his many accomplishments, though, he was proudest of his family: Karl's daughter Lauren was the light of his life, and she loved him too. Wherever he was deployed, she would write to him. During Desert Storm, she sent him a text that read: "Daddy, I have Jesus in my heart."

When she was thirteen, Lauren suffered severe head injuries, which impaired her decision-making ability. Throughout her adolescent years, Lauren made some bad choices: she got involved with drugs, and that led to legal trouble. Things began to look up, though, when Lauren started going to Alcoholics Anonymous meetings. She had been clean and sober for more than a year when, in a moment of bad judgment, Lauren relapsed, overdosed, and died. The light in Karl's life went out. What does Jesus's resurrection mean for Karl Matter?

Karl's crushed spirit and bitter tears are not unlike Mary Magdalene's as she went to the Lord's grave early on the first day of the week. Jesus had transformed Mary: he healed her, he taught her, and she was devoted to him. She believed, as did the other disciples that he was the promised prophet like Moses. They were sure Jesus was the Messiah who would restore the kingdom of Israel to its former glory. In a matter of days, though, those hopes were crushed. Jesus was betrayed by a friend; arrested; condemned; tortured; dragged through the streets; and publicly executed on a Roman cross. It was a painful, humiliating, and slow death.

The Romans crucified criminals to make examples of them. The cross warned others: "If you don't want to end up like that guy, don't act like him." The crucifixion sent Jesus's frightened disciples into hiding! Just a few, like Mary, remained to be close to his spirit a little longer. After such a death, no one thought

Jesus was the Messiah, he was just another failed prophet. God's Anointed wouldn't end up on a cross.

Mary went to the tomb that Sunday morning wanting to be close to her friend one last time. Seeing the tomb open and empty horrified her: the only reasonable conclusion she could draw was that grave robbers or his enemies, had stolen Jesus's body, further defiling it. Pain heaped upon pain.

She ran to Peter and John to report the horror. When they went to the tomb, everything was as Mary said: Jesus's tomb was empty, the burial linens were lying on the ground, and the body was gone. Peter was bewildered; John "believed" something but he didn't quite know what. They went home, leaving a brokenhearted Mary, tears streaming down her face, alone.

Looking into the tomb as she wept, Mary saw two white-clad figures.

"Woman," one of them asked her, "why are you crying?"

She said, "They have taken my Lord away, and I don't know where they put him."

Mary turned and became aware of another in the garden who also asks her: "Woman, why are you crying? Who is it that you're looking for?"

Thinking him to be the gardener, she answered: "Sir, if you've taken him away, let me know where you put him, and I will get him." No questions asked.

One word transformed her life, and with it all of history: "Mary."

The Good Shepherd calls his sheep by name, and they know him! They hear his voice and follow, and he gives them eternal life." She recognized Jesus immediately. "Rabboni," she said. "My great teacher."

"Don't hold on to me," he told her. He still had work to do, and so did she. "Go to my brothers."

The Greek word used here is *apostello*, a verb meaning "to send forth." Jesus sends Mary to bring the good news to his "brothers."

Mary left that cemetery a different woman she knew that the

One who died lives! There was no doubt after Friday that Jesus had died; now she has no doubt that he lives.

Lee Strobel, a Harvard-educated lawyer, journalist, and skeptic, set out to write a book debunking Christ. After painstaking research, Strobel concluded that the resurrection of Jesus Christ is one of the most historically well-documented events of the ancient world. The evidence: his frightened disciples, who ran from Jesus to save their lives, were transformed, in a matter of days, into courageous evangelists. They weren't afraid of Rome, Pilate, or the Temple authorities. They weren't afraid of beatings, imprisonment, or death itself. What changed them? They encountered the Risen Lord. Death had no power over him, or them. "Those who believe in me should live even if they die. And those who live believing in me will never die."

We weep because we fear death in all its manifestations: we cry because of our losses, grief, and pain. We weep because nothing is permanent; in time, all things pass away. Death touches every life, and we can cling to nothing.

Who is it that you are seeking? We live in this world filled with loss, and we seek that which gives our lives and times meaning. Could it be that what we look for is standing right next to us, unrecognized? Only the Risen One can console us and comfort us and restore all that we have lost. Jesus holds it all for us. The moment we believe in him, everything in our life is transformed: our love, our friendships, our families. In Christ, we are a new creation; Jesus's resurrection is his promise that we, who believe in him, will also rise, and that life wins! Always!

Karl shared Lauren's diary with me. It was filled with love for her family and loved ones, faith in God, and genuine struggle with the darkness of drugs and addiction. There was a prayer on every page. On one page, she wrote, "Lord, I don't want to go back to the nightmare of drugs; if I do, I don't want to come back." She belonged to the Good Shepherd. Death could grasp her, but not defeat her. Even though she died, she lives.

Why weep? The One we are looking for abides with us! Now!

Prayer

Risen Lord, we give you thanks and praise for the victory you won for us over slavery to sin and over death itself. It appeared, in the eyes of the world, that you were utterly defeated on the cross: the world had said no to you and all you represented. When you rose from the tomb on the first day of the week, your victory was complete; though the world said no, your Father said yes. It was his will that, on Calvary, you engaged in a cosmic struggle with evil and death. You were faithful to your mission, and the Father was faithful to you. Now we are all your brothers and sisters, made whole by your sacrifice. Give us the courage, Lord, to accept our own crosses with faithfulness and dedication. Keep us close to you and fill us with your Spirit so that, united to you, we too might triumph and rise with you to the newness of life. We ask this through your blood shed for us on the cross. You died, and now you live forever, one with the Father and the Spirit. Amen.

Activity

- Start the day by going to church. Rejoice in the resurrection with other Christians who also have new life in his name.
- Join with friends for a festive Easter dinner. If you aren't hosting that dinner, accept an invitation, or invite friends to dine with you at a restaurant to celebrate this greatest of all days on the Christian Calendar.
- Pray for Christians who are not able to celebrate Easter because of persecution or fear.
- Visit a sick friend who can't get out to celebrate; bring flowers.

Prayer Journal and Notes

Afterword

New Life in Christ

Therefore, if anyone is in Christ, the new creation has come: The old has gone, the new is here!
—2 Corinthians 5:17

The resurrection of Jesus occurred more than two thousand years ago. He has gone from an immediate presence among his disciples and has become the one we remember when we gather around a table, break bread, and share wine in his memory. Is he less with us now?

Faith would answer no. He is with us differently but powerfully.

In the garden, Jesus told Mary not to cling to him but to go and say to his disciples that he was ascending to the Father—his Father and theirs.

We can't cling to the physical presence of Christ either because the resurrection changes everything. It transformed the physical Jesus from a brutalized corpse into a glorified body, shining and unencumbered by walls or miles. He appeared to Mary and the others with a message of shalom—of a peace that the world cannot give, God's own peace. Jesus mission of reconciliation was accomplished, the victory had been won, death had been conquered, and with it all, it's allies: sickness, pestilence, violence, hatred, and war. All the power of this world, a power that inevitably leads to death, was overcome forever when Jesus came forth from the tomb alive and radiant with the Glory of God.

If Jesus's resurrection was for him alone, it would be amazing but not significant for us all these years later. It would have changed him, but not us. His victory wasn't for him alone, it was to save and transform all of us. Like him, we are subject to death, but are not overcome by it. For the Christian, death is swallowed up in the victory Jesus won for us on Calvary, and our eternal life is guaranteed by his resurrection. When he emerged from the tomb on the third day, we emerged with him.

Our new life in Christ begins the moment we embrace the Risen One as Lord and Savior.

In baptism, we go, ritually, into the water, which represents his tomb. We die to the world when we embrace Christ; we die to its lies and lures; we die to its false promises and empty pleasures. We die to ourselves and our petty egos. Unless we die to ourselves, the Lord taught, we cannot save our lives. Only when we die with Christ do we have eternal life—and we have it immediately.

We still die, as did the first Christians whose faith has been bequeathed to us through successive generations of believers. To this day, there are martyrs for the faith, still giving their lives as they profess their faith in the Risen One. Christians die daily—in accidents, hospitals, and their beds. Death has not taken a holiday since the resurrection. We still have wars, sickness, and disasters of every kind. But in this we are conquerors. Death can end the life of our bodies but cannot take the vital Spirit that forever has been entrusted to the Father by the Son in the Spirit.

The Spirit, sent to us by the Lord to be his abiding presence with us, another Advocate, remains by our sides through it all. This Spirit is with us from the beginning of our lives, loving, guiding, prodding, luring us toward the Father. The Spirit opens our eyes to the teaching and meaning of God's Christ. The Spirit is with us when we draw our last breath, as it was when we drew our first.

When that last breath is drawn, life is changed, not ended.

Because of Christ's victory on Calvary, death and suffering can never have the last word. Life wins!

The reality of our victory in Christ is captured by the English poet and pastor, John Donne, in his sonnet "Death Be Not Proud":

> Death, be not proud, though some have called thee
> Mighty and dreadful, for thou are not so;
> For those whom thou think'st thou dost overthrow
> Die not, poor death, nor yet canst thou kill me.
> From rest and sleep, which but thy pictures be,
> Much pleasure; then from thee much more must flow,
> And soonest our best men with thee do go,
> Rest of their bones, and soul's delivery.
> Thou'art slave to fate, chance, kings, and desperate men,
> And dost with poison, war, and sickness dwell,
> And poppy' or charms can make us sleep as well
> And better than thy stroke; why swell'st thou then?
> One short sleep past, we wake eternally,
> And death shall be no more; Death, thou shalt die.[9]

---

[9] John Donne, Holy Sonnets: "Death, Be Not Proud," Poetry Foundation website, retrieved from https://www.poetryfoundation.org/poems/44107/holy-sonnets-death-be-not-proud.

About the Author

Richard Hasselbach is pastor of Clarkstown Reformed Church in West Nyack, New York. He has pastored churches in both New York and Florida. Rev. Hasselbach is a graduate of Siena College (B.A.) and holds advanced degrees from both Boston College Law School (J.D.) and Fordham University (Ph.D.).

Active in the Community, Rev. Hasselbach sits on the Clarkstown, NY Board of Ethics and the Rockland County Human Rights Commission. He has taught at St. Bonaventure University and Mercy College.

He is an animal lover and is owned by two small dogs: Oliver, a 2 year old Coton d'Tulear, and Faux Pas, an 11 year old Bichon Frise.

CPSIA information can be obtained
at www.ICGtesting.com
Printed in the USA
BVHW040048220322
631714BV00006B/16